TALKING
WITH GOD

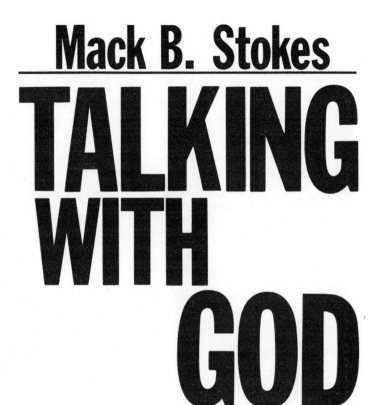

Mack B. Stokes

TALKING WITH GOD

ABINGDON PRESS

Nashville

TALKING WITH GOD

This book is printed on acid-free paper.

Library of Congress Cataloging-in-Publication Data

Stokes, Mack B.
  Talking with God: a guide to prayer/Mack B. Stokes.
  p. cm.
  ISBN 0-687-40999-3 (alk. paper)
  1. Prayer.   I. Title.
BV215.S82   1989
248.3'2—dc20   89-33140
                                                      CIP

Scripture quotations, unless otherwise noted, are from the Revised
Standard Version of the Bible, copyright 1946, 1952, 1971 by the Division
of Christian Education of the National Council of Churches of Christ in the
USA. Used by permission.

Those noted KJV are from the King James Version of the Bible.

MANUFACTURED BY THE PARTHENON PRESS AT
NASHVILLE, TENNESSEE, UNITED STATES OF AMERICA

To my daughter,
Elsie Pauline,
for her many valuable editoral suggestions.

Contents

Chapter One
INTRODUCTION

Chapter Two
PRAYER IN THE BIBLICAL HERITAGE

Chapter Three
PRAYER AND SOME BASIC PROBLEMS

Chapter Four
PRAYER AND CREATIVE LIVING

Introduction

PRAYER AS THE HEART OF RELIGION

Religion is the dimension of our experience that concerns the *relationship* between *God* and *us*. What does *God* have to do with us? What is His purpose for us? What do we have to do with God? How can we open our souls to God and receive His blessings? How can we work together with God? How are we related to others through God? What does God have in mind for us after death? These are religious questions.

Why are they distinctively religious? Because these questions are asked in no other areas of human life. For example, in business such questions are not asked unless the people involved happen to be religious. They are not the questions labor asks. We do not ask them when we are developing skills to do a job and make a living. Public schools, colleges, and universities do not exist to ask them. Museums of art, libraries, sports arenas have their roles; but they do not raise religious questions. Romance, too, though one of the important human interests, is not by itself alone religious.

So religion is a unique sphere of life. And prayer is the heart of religion. For in prayer we stop talking about religion and enter into a relationship with God. Prayer, in its highest form, is communion and encounter with God.

When we pray we sense the presence of God. We feel ourselves drawn to the One who made us for Himself. We feel our utter dependence on God and stand in awe of Him. At the same time, we have the mysterious awareness of the Father's love. We know that He who made us loves us. He who knows us cares for us. In prayer we know that God calls us to the new life. God not only knows and loves us: He summons us to a great destiny. And, in our ongoing pilgrimage through this present life, we receive from God the power to see life through with joy and hope.

In prayer, then, we feel this strangely profound experience of awe and dread mingled with adoration and love. We know that without God we would be nothing. We are aware of our creatureliness. We bow before our Creator. At the same time, we know that with God our flimsy existence becomes real and authentic. We lift up our hearts to our Maker and Redeemer.

Religion, then, far from being just another experience, is another *kind* of experience. Therefore, it must never be placed alongside of our many other kinds of experiences. Nevertheless, through prayer all other areas of life may be influenced and enriched. In moments of prayer—sometimes gradually and sometimes suddenly—we become aware of the ineptness of any of the offerings of this world to satisfy our deepest needs. For only God can probe the depths of our being and meet those needs which cry out for an answer. In prayer we break through the boundaries of this present realm and enter into a living relationship with the Holy One who is beyond yet within those boundaries.

Without religion this connection with the Ultimate Ground of our being is left out. And without this connection we cannot be fully human. We are like creatures living yet only partly living. Without this link with God we are reduced to inauthentic forms of existence. Our life lacks any enduring foundation. And we feel like passing whiffs of insignificance. Augustine knew this when he wrote what is perhaps the greatest sentence ever uttered outside the Bible: "Thou hast made us for thyself, O God, and our souls are restless till they rest in thee."

By virtue of our nature as human beings, we are endowed with a capacity for responding to God. This capacity, like other capacities, comes to expression as life goes on. It is nurtured or stifled, as the case may be, by environmental factors. But it is no more created by them than is the capacity for arithmetic, music, art, or athletics. It presses forward through all kinds of environmental circumstances. The history of religion shows that this inborn capacity for God longs for utterance. Various phrases have been used to identify this human endowment. Some have called it our religious nature. Others have referred to it as our religious intuition, or religious *a priori*, or religious sentiment.

There is much evidence supporting the idea that human beings have a kind of intuitive awareness of God. We perceive that the finite points to the Infinite, the passing calls for the Enduring, and the imperfect cries out for the Perfect. We are always observing things that come into being and pass away. Flowers wither away and die. Cars run down and have to be traded away. Our dogs and cats, though precious, grow old and die. We ourselves join all those creatures great and small which come into existence on this earth and then pass away. So is it with all our attachments. Friends come and go. When we die, our fondness for carefully selected pieces of furniture, or houses, or farms, vanishes like passing gusts of wind. These grim certainties are perpetual reminders of our finitude. In our human situation we perceive, by a kind of direct insight, that God is and that He alone abides amid the things that come and go. Often this experience emerges as a kind of dim consciousness of the Infinite. And sometimes it bursts forth into an inspired prayer of absolute faith in God.

This is what Henry F. Lyte (1793–1847) must have felt when he prayed:

> Swift to its close ebbs out life's little day;
> Earth's joys grow dim, its glories pass away;
> Change and decay in all around I see;
> O thou who changest not, abide with me.

In prayer this mysterious, intuitive certainty comes home to us. For as we pray we feel ourselves to be in direct and life-giving relationship with the One who is from everlasting to everlasting. It is here, then, that this mysterious unique sphere of the religious comes alive for us and in us. For God is known, loved, adored, felt, and responded to when we open our souls to Him. God communes with us and we with Him. In prayer God meets us where we are and summons us to the new life. And there we begin to see that everything we are and do receives enduring meaning and glory from the God who made us for Himself.

WHAT IS PRAYER?

All true prayer is person-to-Person communion and encounter with God. It involves trustful dependence, gratitude, adoration, confession, petition, openness to God, decision, and love. It includes the sustained desire to understand and do God's will in spite of counteracting impulses. During certain moments of prayer, the word "communion" is inadequate. I refer to those moments when God encounters us and we encounter God. I have in mind those times when, like the Psalmists and Jeremiah, we pour out our souls, our fears, our despair, our struggles, and, as a result, are moved into a more vital relationship with God. In prayer also there is an awareness of how God is affected by us—His displeasure with us, His enjoyment of us. For God Himself is hurt by our wrong attitudes and failures. And He is blessed as we are blessed. This mysterious fellowship with God, like all true friendships, is an end-in-itself. It is more than that. Nevertheless, it stands in its own right and is self-authenticating.

Often prayer begins by asking God for things. Petition is a basic element of prayer. But it is only one such element. There are many levels of our petitions. They may be crude and petty or refined and magnanimous. And the quality of our prayer-life can be measured in part by the quality of our petitions. When reduced to mere selfish entreaty, prayer may become a source of doubt. Why? For two reasons. First, as life goes on, we learn that God does not always grant our requests. If a mother prays for her son to recover from a serious illness, and he dies, her faith may be shaken. Second, doubts arise when we think primarily of prayer as petition because we lose sight of the deeper meaning of prayer, namely, communion and encounter with God.

It is still true, however, as Jesus taught (Matt. 7:7), that entreaty has its worthy place in prayer. Deeply rooted in our Christian heritage is the conviction that we are to make our requests known to God (see Phil. 4:6). Our Lord's Prayer contains petitions relative to both our physical needs and our moral and spiritual needs. Therefore, no understanding of prayer can be adequate which does not include petition in it.

Some people think of prayer as ritual. They think chiefly of the words used, the forms followed, the routines practiced. Prayer means "saying prayers," reading prayers, or counting prayers. In its cruder forms this understanding of prayer borders on magic. For it is often supposed that we can affect God by going through certain routines. For many devout people who pray, ritual may lead them into authentic experiences of communion and encounter with God. Nevertheless, there is always the danger of stressing formal exactness more than the living person-to-Person relationship with God.

Still others have given us wide varieties of definitions of prayer. In each of these there is real groping for a deeper understanding. Some say that prayer is a quest for truth. Prayer is understanding. Others say that prayer is "the soul's sincere desire, uttered or unexpressed." Kant spoke of it as a "heartfelt wish."

Again, there is the view that prayer is emotion. It is feeling a certain way toward God and the universe. For a large number of people, prayer is contemplation or meditation. And for others it is simply aspiration or the longing and reaching for the ideal.

Each of these ways of looking at prayer has some truth in it. But each fails to grasp the essential reality of prayer, namely, communion and encounter with God. Prayer involves ritual but only as a means to communion and to the life-giving relationship with God. Prayer implies the quest for understanding, but understanding by itself misses the unique dimension of the *experienced* presence of God. Prayer, on one side, is desire. But we have all sorts of desires. Desire is not connected with prayer until it aims toward God and is fulfilled in God. Contemplation, meditation, and aspiration are all factors in creative prayer. But, by themselves, they are merely human processes. They become living forces in prayer when we feel we are in the presence of God.

Many people today fix their attention on the merely human. Their vision of God, if it exists at all, tends to be blurred or obscured by their ceaseless study of themselves, their problems, and their surroundings. Therefore, they miss the mysterious depths of Christian experience. The quality of our experiences is largely determined by the quality of the realities we encounter. When we see an ant hill, we feel one thing. When we stand before the Alps, we feel another. *Vast oceans roll between those whose experiences are confined to the merely human and those who feel that they are in the presence of God.*

From prayer in the biblical heritage we receive many blessings. One of the most precious of these is *the sense of belonging to God.* We know our true identity. We are no longer mere products of nature. Nor are we just members of a family or community. We are not simply psychological creatures with all sorts of tendencies, impressions, and impulses. Rather, in prayer we are given the marvelous awareness that we are the children of God. Everyone knows the painful experience of being left out. We know what it is *not* to belong. In prayer we experience the overwhelming sense of belonging to our heavenly Father who has chosen us to be His own precious creatures.

The blessings of the life of prayer are not merely momentary: they come from growth in the practice of prayer. All authentic men and women of prayer made it a lifelong process. For them it meant pressing forward in understanding God's holy purpose for them and in responding to the divine summons. In this total process they became increasingly aware of God's delight in this divine-human relationship.

The inevitable fruit of this person-to-Person communion and encounter with God is a resounding yes to God's call to let Him do His work through us. And, of course, this means service to our fellow human beings. Prayer is communion and encounter with God in which the soul turns toward God and responds to His will. Since character and conduct emerge from our profound inner experiences and relationships, it follows as the night the day that creative service will flow from the life of prayer. For God is not only to be adored and enjoyed; He is to be obeyed. God has overwhelmingly important goals which he strives to realize through us. In the life of prayer and service Jesus Christ is our Source and Model. Through prayer the Holy Spirit acts within us to fill us with the love of Christ. And in this way we are given by grace what Wesley called that "inward holiness" which leads to "outward holiness."

WHY PRAY?

There are three primary reasons why we should pray. The first is that God commands it. The second is that our human needs require it. The third is that God advances His kingdom by it. Let us consider these.

God wants us to pray, so He commands it. Our Creator knows what is best for us. He alone is ever mindful of the purpose for which He created us and placed us on this earth. God made us to enter into the life-giving relationship with Himself by faith. And this involves prayer. In the Old Testament, God's call to prayer comes primarily through the example of the great leaders of Israel. All of them—from Abraham to Moses to Deborah to Hannah to Samuel to David to Elijah to Job and to the prophets—were people of prayer. As we shall see in chapter 5, the Psalmists gave people some of the grand words for prayer.

When we come to the New Testament, we find that Jesus and the apostles called us to pray both by their example and precept. Jesus led the way by his own life of prayer. He was praying at the time of his baptism (Luke 3:21). He prayed during the forty days when he went into the wilderness and was tempted by the devil (cf. Matt. 4:1-11; and the parallel passages in Mark and Luke). Often he withdrew from the crowds to pray (cf. Luke 5:16; 9:18, 28; 11:1. He prayed all night before choosing his disciples (Luke 6:12-16). He prayed for Peter that he might not be destroyed by

Satan (Luke 22:31-32). He prayed for his followers—including those in succeeding generations (John 17:20). He prayed at Gethsemane (Luke 22:41-44). He prayed on the cross (Luke 23:34).

Jesus commanded his followers to pray. Knowing the awesome power of temptation, he said, "Watch and pray that you may not enter into temptation" (Mark 14:38; and parallel passages in Matt. and Luke). He commanded his disciples to pray for God to send laborers into the harvest (Matt. 9:38; Luke 10:2). Among the Master's important commands was to pray for one's enemies. In addition, Jesus commanded his followers to pray the special prayer which he taught them.

The Apostles became leaders in the call to prayer. And Paul summarized this when he said, "Pray without ceasing" (I Thess. 5:17 KJV). In a true sense, the whole Bible has been for Christians the Word of God calling them to the life of prayer. One of the most important reasons for reading the Bible devotionally is that it helps us to know that we are in the presence of God, for He speaks to us in His holy Word. And, through the Bible, God provides that spiritual atmosphere in which we can enter into the living communion and encounters with God.

How easily we forget that we were made for God and that without God we grope in the dark! God has revealed His unalterable reasons for calling us to pray and even for commanding us to do so. In every era people have been distracted because there are in our human nature gravitational pulls away from God. Because of this human condition—as well as because of other forces in us and around us—people in all ages have turned away from God and gone their own ways. But ours is in notable respects an age of distraction. The mass media, cars, highways, airplanes, and many other technological advances provide countless attractions that lure us away from God. Therefore, in these times we are especially prone to forget that the most compelling reason for praying is that God commands it.

Before taking this thought further, several clarifying comments are needed. For one thing, we need to keep clearly in mind *Who* commands us to pray and why. He is not a tyrannical cosmic despot ordering us about as though we were slaves. We are rightly repulsed by the idea of a divine tyrant who demands that we bow before him. The Holy One who summons us to pray is our Creator who called us into being. God made us, knows us, loves us, strives with us, delights in our existence and in our full humanity. So our Maker, who loves us most and knows us best, commands us to pray. As soon as we see this command as God's way of seeking us and longing for our best, our whole attitude changes.

Another insight needs to be added. The word "command" does not mean "a legalistic demand." Rather, it is a personal summons based on God's concern for us. It is not merely an order addressed to society. As the Bible teaches, it is an intimately personal word addressed to each one of us. God summons you and me to pray. Through Jesus Christ, this comes to us as God's personal invitation. It is an expression of his interest and love. Our part, then, is to respond by praying and growing in the practice of prayer.

Furthermore, God's command to pray is not made once and for all. It is not to be understood as something carved in stone, fixed and rigid. On the contrary, the command to pray is living, personal, ever new and fresh. For God always takes into account the vital human interests of each new day and every new situation.

Another thought bears directly on God's summons to pray. This is the idea that even God is enriched by our prayers. He delights in our responsiveness and rejoices in our cooperation. God enjoys communion and encounter with us. Does this sound like some far-out new teaching? On the contrary, it is an often overlooked biblical teaching about God. Otherwise, why is there the talk in the Old Testament about God's wrath, His disappointment with the people of Israel and with particular individuals? And why was Jesus weeping over Jerusalem or hanging on a cross? The only adequate answer must include the thought that God delights in His children's appropriate responses to Him and, otherwise, is profoundly hurt and saddened by their wanderings from Him.

The second reason for praying is that our human nature requires it. People often find it hard to understand their deeper moral and spiritual needs. They cover up those needs and blindly refuse to face them. As life moves on, these deeper needs make themselves felt. Sometimes during a crisis we feel the need of God. And crises are sure to come. In sickness we become aware of how feeble we are. Death is the grim reminder of our absolute dependence on God. The breakdown of character, affecting both ourselves and those who love us, opens our eyes to the need for God. The loss of work and business failures makes us think about deeper values.

The stark truth is this: As wonderful as our life on earth may be, it is fraught with uncertainty, failure, pain, and tragedy. Even when everything seems to be going our way, we still know that nothing which this world has to offer—however attractive—can satisfy the deep mysterious longing for God.

> Amidst our plenty, something still,
> To me, to thee, to him is wanting!

People can have great wealth, extensive properties, a good marriage, children, and the added gratifications from art, literature, culture, athletic diversions, and still feel a sense of emptiness until they lift up their hearts in prayer and know that they belong to God.

Under many of the circumstances of life, our need for God is so overwhelming that we cannot help praying. William James, the well-known Harvard psychologist and philosopher, summarized the situation in such a way that he still speaks to us: "We hear in these days of scientific enlightenment, a great deal of discussion about the efficacy of prayer; and many reasons are given us why we should not pray; whilst others are given us why we should. But in all this very little is said of the reason why we *do* pray, which is simply that we cannot *help* praying" (*Principles of Psychology*, I, 316).

The basic point is that no one can struggle most productively through life's baffling circumstances without God's help. And none can rise to the highest levels of full humanity without divine assistance. If we are strong, we still need God's immeasurably greater resources to make us stronger. If we are weak, our weakness is made strong by God's grace (cf. II Cor. 12:9). If we are cruel, hostile, anxious, and mixed up, our inner life can be transformed by the creative dynamics of the love of Christ. If we become weary in the tasks of life, God summons us to pray so that we may receive new resources for creative living.

The third reason for praying is implied in the first two. God commands it and our human needs require it so that through prayer God's holy kingdom can be realized in us and through us on earth. Much more than prayer is needed to advance God's work in the world. It takes the presence of the Risen Christ in us. It takes Pentecost. It takes the wisdom that the love of Christ implies. It takes people who have so opened their hearts to God in prayer that they are eager to identify God's will for them and to move where God is leading them. It requires policy decisions. It requires Christian marriages and family life. It requires institution-building. It requires Christian character in business, labor, the professions, the mass media, government, and in the total life in community. Our own best resources need to interact with God's grace for the highest glory of God and the blessing of human beings.

CHAPTER TWO

Prayer in the Biblical Heritage

BIBLICAL PERSONALISM AS NORMATIVE

The Bible is our primary source and norm in understanding prayer. It is our guide also in the practice of prayer. No other sacred writings compare with it in the emphasis on prayer as communion and encounter with God. By searching other writings we may find scattered references which are comparable to the emphasis the biblical writers placed on prayer. But they are few and far between. Friedrich Heiler states:

> In the exposition of prayer in personal religion it is almost exclusively Biblical and Christian personalities that have to be taken into account. Christianity, including the prophetic religion of the Old Testament, is 'the peculiar home of personal prayer. . . .' To be sure, prayer is the essential utterance of all the religions of the world; it is not an exclusively Christian but a universally human phenomenon. But the personal *life of prayer*, free and living intercourse with

God, has its native abode in Christianity as it has nowhere else in the entire history of religion.

Heiler lists some exceptions to this in non-Christian religions and adds that the records of their prayers can be regarded only as parallels alongside the incomparably richer testimonies of those in the biblical heritage (Friedrich Heiler, *Prayer* [New York: Oxford University Press, 1958], pp. 119-21).

The basic reason for this foundational role of the Bible in relation to prayer is seen in the personalism of the Bible. The Bible is personalistic from beginning to end. By this I mean three things. First and foremost, there is the biblical revelation on God as the Ultimate Personal Spirit. Second, there is the biblical revelation on human beings as finite personal spirits or souls. Third, there is the revelation on prayer as interpersonal communion and encounter with God. Our finite souls are communing with and encountering God in person-to-Person experiences. The I-Thou relationship is at the heart of the biblical teaching on prayer.

There are two notable ways of moving outside the orbit of biblical meanings of prayer. On the one hand, we can affirm the role of prayer as a purely subjective phenomenon. This reduces prayer to human beings talking to themselves. According to this view, there may be some value in prayer as meditation, self-analysis, and quiet reflection. But there is no communion and encounter with God, no person-to-Person relationship. Consequently, in denying the reality of the personal God, the biblical teaching on prayer is reduced to an illusion. Some people fall into this kind of thinking by viewing prayer as psychological projection. That is, they say that we project our thoughts and merely imagine the reality and presence of God. Others do this by calling prayer a case of wishful thinking. There are varieties of these subjectivistic theories. In response to all such views, I would say that, where prayer is concerned, everything depends on the reality of God as the Ultimate Personal Spirit. If God is—as the Bible teaches and our best thinking confirms—then the biblical understanding of prayer rests on solid foundations. Besides this, it is unreasonable to sweep away, on the basis of a psychological theory, what has been confirmed in the experiences of millions of people throughout the centuries.

On the other hand, we can move away from the biblical teaching on prayer by thinking of God in impersonal terms. As to God, some have said that God is the Ultimate One. Others have thought of God as Being-in-itself. Still others have urged that God is Cosmic Process. Each of these—and many others similar to them—has the merit of affirming the reality of some kind of Ultimate Being or Process called God. But none of them opens the way to the kind of person-to-Person encounter of which the Bible speaks. On the basis of these views of God as impersonal Being or Process, there have been mystical types of prayer. For example, some have moved toward absorption into the divine Being. And others have ascended the ladder of prayer to behold the glory and beauty of God as abstract Goodness. The history of mystical types of prayer has its value and glory. But, however meaningful in the lives of Christians and others, it takes people away from the primary focus of the Bible on prayer as the I-Thou relationship and personal communion and encounter with God.

One of the finest philosophical statements I know on the idea of God as the Ultimate Personal Spirit is Borden P. Bowne's chapter entitled "The Failure of Impersonalism" *(Personalism,* chapter 5). I agree with William Earnest Hocking, who said: "There is no more powerful and convincing chapter in American metaphysical writing than that of Bowne on 'the failure of impersonalism.'" Bowne was writing not on impersonalism in relation to prayer, but on the failure of impersonalism to lead us to an ultimate causal explanation of the world which we know to exist. Nevertheless, that chapter affirms the reality of the Personal God whose volitional agency alone is adequate to account for the world. And, though the biblical revelation by itself is sufficient, this opens the way, on intellectual grounds, to the reality of prayer as communion and encounter with God.

For those who want to turn prayer into a strategy for using God for their selfish ends, the Bible will have to be laid aside. For those who are interested in prayer as mystical absorption into the divine Being, the Bible will not be their source-book. Similarly, for those who think of prayer as a ladder of ascent toward God, the Bible will be only one among various guides. And for those who want the by-products of prayer—mental health, emotional healing, positive thinking, peace of mind, and even love—without the demands implied in the encounter with God, the Bible will have little appeal.

But for those who think of prayer as a responsible person-to-Person relationship with God—encompassing the full ranges and depths of our souls—the Bible is the supreme source and guide. Therefore, the Christian leaders in the life of prayer have immersed themselves in the atmosphere and spirit of the Bible. This is especially evident in their devotional writings and practices. It is evident also when we survey the prayer books of the various churches. Through these prayer books, which received their inspiration and direction from the Bible, prayer as person-to-Person communion and encounter with God has been kept alive from generation to generation in local churches throughout the world.

Against this background, consider with me five ways in which the biblical writers—with their intrinsic personalism—have influenced the prayer-life of Christians. Many other items might be mentioned. But consider five. The first was their awareness of being in the presence of the God who mysteriously called them into being. Along with this, the biblical writers knew that God made them for a purpose. So they were not only to adore God; they were to obey God.

Second, the biblical writers were keenly aware of being in the presence of the *holy* God. And they knew that this holy God required of them love, justice, mercy, and peacemaking. This realization has had a profound effect upon Christians in their prayer-life across the centuries.

A third factor in the influence of the biblical writers upon succeeding generations of Christians was their practice of prayer in community. Their personal encounters with God were experienced communally. This is seen in the Old Testament in the covenantal ties binding people together under the God of Abraham, Isaac, and Jacob. In the New Testament this communal experience centered in the presence of the Holy Spirit who bound Christians together under their common Lord.

A fourth influence from the biblical writers came to utterance in the New Testament. I have in mind the connection between prayer and Jesus Christ. Jesus Himself established this when He taught His disciples to pray in His name (John 14:13-14, 15:16; 16: 23-24; cf. Eph. 5:20; Col. 3:17). Jesus Christ is the vine and His followers the branches. This focus on Christ set the standard for the quality of Christian prayer. And this saved Christians from those misguided expressions of "spirituality" which do not reflect the essential purity and good will of the Master.

Fifth, the apostles and other early Christians influenced later Christians in prayer because they felt the presence of the Holy Spirit as a dynamic reality in prayer. Far from being impersonal, the Holy Spirit was known and experienced by them to be personal. The illuminating presence, guidance, and assistance of the Holy Spirit profoundly and mysteriously enriched the apostolic experience of prayer. Through the Holy Spirit the apostles and others held fast to Christ as central in their prayers. And through the assistance of the Holy Spirit, they heard again and again the Risen Lord's call to give themselves in the service of others. And this too has profoundly influenced the prayer-life of Christians by inspiring them to see the unbreakable connection between authentic prayer and service. The apostles saw, as none before them, that the purpose of the holy God for all human beings was to realize moral and spiritual values in community under the Lordship of Jesus Christ. Inward holiness produces outward holiness.

These five elements in the influence of the biblical writers on succeeding generations of Christians are concretely seen in the prayer books, hymnals, song books, anthems, liturgies, and sermons of the churches which bear the name of Jesus Christ. They are seen also in the lives of Christians.

THE PSALMISTS AS TEACHERS ON PRAYER

The Book of Psalms contains a wide variety of religious poetry. Some of the psalms are hymns of adoration and praise. A few contain communal lamentations; many more, individual lamentations. Some are psalms of thanksgiving. In addition, there are psalms pertaining to reigning kings, or to Mt. Zion, or to cultic ceremonies. Psalms 1 and 37 have been called wisdom poetry.

When we consider the variety of themes in the Book of Psalms, we see clearly that some of them do not give us guidance in understanding prayer. There are psalms that even plunge into the depths of vindictiveness. Nevertheless, it was with good reason that the earliest Christians joined the people of Israel in recognizing the glorious devotional heritage of the Psalter. Christians learned from their experiences in the Temple and synagogues and used Israel's Psalms in their own services of worship. Almost from the beginning, in their congregations Christians sang with words from the Psalter (see Eph. 5:19). One scholar has said that ninety-three passages from the Psalms are quoted in the New Testament (see *The Interpreter's Bible*, vol. 4, p. 16).

The most important psalms which bear directly on prayer as communion and encounter with God are those which express adoration, thanksgiving, lamentation, repentance, soul-searching, and trust in God's mercy and help. Let us now consider five important contributions of the psalmists to the development of prayer in the biblical heritage.

(1) They gave sublime utterance to the greatness and glory of God as the Ultimate Personal Spirit. We are told that even before Creation God is "from everlasting to everlasting" (90:2). The psalmists lifted up the greatness and glory of God as the Creator who "stretched out the heavens like a tent, and . . . set the earth on its foundations." God is the One who makes "the grass to grow for the cattle, and plants for man to cultivate" (104:2, 5, 14). It is this God "who by understanding made the heavens" and "spread out the earth upon the waters" (136:5-6).

> O Lord, how manifold are thy
> works!
> In wisdom hast thou made them
> all. (104:24)

The psalmists were not philosophical minds. Yet, by their inspired intuitions, they gave poetic utterance to what Borden P. Bowne, founder of American philosophical personalism, wrote when he said, "In all our thinking, when critically scrutinized, we find self-conscious and active intelligence the presupposition not only of our knowledge but of the world of objects as well" (*Personalism* [Boston: Houghton Mifflin Co., 1908], p. 27). This implies that mind (wisdom) is at both ends of the line. For what God created in wisdom, He enables us to understand with our limited God-given intelligence.

The psalmists also gave sublime utterance to the greatness and glory of God as the Holy One whose "steadfast love endures for ever." Here the ethical monotheism of Israel comes into clear focus. And this sense of the absolute goodness of God is organically connected with His marvelous love which led to the covenant with Abraham.

Much has been said about the communal function of the Psalms. And it is beyond question that this was the main use of many of them. One of the most conspicuous examples of this is found in Psalm 136. Here, the following formula is repeated—as if responsively by the congregation—after successive statements on the mighty acts of God in creation and history: ". . . for his steadfast love endures for ever." The psalmists would not let Israel forget this marvelous love of God. Whether for their communal worship or their personal life, that formula, or one similar to it, was affirmed throughout the Book of Psalms. It was a mighty, recurring theme in the poetic imagination of Israel (21:7; 25:10; 26:3; 32:10; 51:1; 63:3; 86:13; 89:14; 100:5; 103:4, 11, 17; 106:1; 107:1, 31; 108:4; 109:21; 117:2; 118:1-4, 29; 119:76, 149, 159; 130:7; 138:2; 147:11).

The affirmation of the greatness and glory of God—both as Creator and Sustainer of the universe and as the Holy One who loves His children forever—has had a profound influence on the devotional and prayer life of Jews and Christians throughout the centuries.

(2) One of the most obvious effects of the psalmists' vision of God is in the call to prayers of adoration,

praise, and thanksgiving. For it was that vision which led them to give to the whole world some of the most magnificent words of adoration ever uttered. And when, after more than 2,000 years, we strive for words which express our sense of wonder and awe in the presence of God, we find ourselves pouring forth the words of the psalmists. They have taught us to adore God, to praise God, and to be filled with gratitude to God. Consider the following words which have been woven into our public and private prayers:

> O Lord, our Lord,
>   how majestic is thy name in all
>   the earth! (8:9)

> Let the peoples praise thee, O God;
>   let all the peoples praise thee! (67:5)

> Every day I will bless thee,
>   and praise thy name for ever and
>   ever.
> Great is the Lord, and greatly to be
>   praised,
>   and his greatness is unsearchable. (145:2-3)

(3) At the same time the psalmists contributed to prayer in the biblical heritage by teaching us that God is altogether approachable. They showed us that God hears our prayers (40:6; 65:2; 116:1-2; 145:18), and they said that God is directly and graciously accessible. Very little is found in the Book of Psalms about making blood sacrifices and offerings to God for our sins. God pardons those who humbly and truly

confess their sins "for [his] name's sake" (25:11; 79:9). For "the sacrifice acceptable to God is a broken spirit" (51:17; see 32:5; 40:6). The psalmist knew that congregations and holy places contribute significantly to devotional life. But they knew also that God was already present within their own souls and ready to understand, to forgive, to empower. They *sensed* the presence of God and invited others to do so (34:8; 119:103).

Because they knew that God is directly accessible and approachable, the psalmists felt free to pour out their hearts to God. They reflected the many moods and struggles of people so fully that St. Augustine rightly called the Book of Psalms "an anatomy of the parts of the soul." There are more than forty psalms of individual lamentations. (As examples, see 4–7; 42–43; 55; 64; 69; 88; 130; and 142.) As they brought their deepest needs to God, mysteriously they found themselves experiencing the sustaining presence of God.

> In peace I will both lie down and
> sleep;
> for thou alone, O Lord, makest
> me dwell in safety. (4:8)

> Why are you cast down, O my soul,
> and why are you disquieted
> within me?
> Hope in God; for I shall again
> praise him,
> my help and my God. (42:11; 43:5)

> Cast your burden on the Lord,
> and he will sustain you;

> he will never permit
> the righteous to be moved. (55:22)

Some have said that the many psalms which use the personal pronouns "I," "me," "my," actually imply a corporate or communal relationship with God. For, so it is said, the people of Israel thought of their communities as being individuals or corporate entities. I cannot accept this view. In those psalms, almost without exception, the personal I-Thou relationship is self-evident. For example, the Twenty-third Psalm, though not a prayer, clearly expresses the thought that God is like a good shepherd to the inspired individual who wrote it. And the continuing glory of that psalm lies in the souls of the millions of people who feel the same caring love of God for them as solitary individuals.

Psalm 139:1-18, 23-24 is one of the greatest prayers which reflects this I-Thou relationship between God and a human being. The psalmist is keenly aware that God knows him through and through. God knew him before he was born and "knit [him] together in [his] mother's womb." God is acquainted in intricate detail with all his ways. So, in the end, he cries to God, saying:

> Search me, O God, and know my
> heart!
> Try me and know my thoughts!
> And see if there be any wicked
> way in me,
> and lead me in the way ever-
> lasting! (139:23-24)

(4) Again, one of the greatest contributions of the psalmists to prayer in the biblical heritage is seen in their inspired words, images, and model prayers. There is a mysterious power about their words and images. Even in translation, we feel this. Augustine experienced it when he wrote: "What utterances I used to send up unto Thee in those Psalms, and how was I inflamed towards Thee by them" (*Confessions*, IX, iv). How our souls are moved to adoration and praise when we sing!

> Bless the Lord, O my soul;
>> and all that is within me,
>>> bless his holy name! (103:1)

> This is the day which the Lord has
>> made;
>> let us rejoice and be glad in it. (118:24)

The psalmists' many words of thanksgiving provided the inspiration for Luther's insight: "The best way to lift the mind to God is to acknowledge and ponder past blessings" (*Luther's Works*, vol. 10, p. 45).

In times of deep despair what words can more perfectly express how we feel than these?

> Out of the depths I cry to
>> thee, O Lord!
>> Lord, hear my voice!
> Let thy ears be attentive
>> to the voice of my supplications! (130:1-2)

Where can we go to find more beautifully meaningful words in which to pray the sinner's prayer than these?

> Have mercy on me, O God,
> according to thy steadfast love;
> according to thy abundant mercy
> blot out my transgressions.
> Wash me thoroughly from my
> inquity,
> and cleanse me from my sin! (51:1-2)

And consider the following lines—out of many others—which have provided thoughts, words, and images for the prayer-life of millions:

The Lord is my light and my
salvation;
whom shall I fear? (27:1)

My times are in thy hand. (31:15)

Fret not yourself because of
the wicked. (37:1)

My soul thirsts for God,
for the living God. (42:2)

Lead thou me
to the rock that is higher than I. (61:2)

O taste and see that the Lord is
good! (34:8)

Be still and know that I am God. (46:10)

If I take the wings of the morning
and dwell in the uttermost parts
of the sea,

even there thy hand shall lead me,
and thy right hand shall hold me. (139:9-10)

And who shall stand in his holy
place?
He who has clean hands and a pure
heart (24:3-4)

So teach us to number our days
that we may apply our hearts unto wisdom. (90:12
KJV)

I will pay my vows to the Lord
in the presence of all his people. (116:14, 18).

The Lord sets the prisoners free. (146:7)

Pray for the peace of Jerusalem! (122:6)

These and other words from the psalmists have
been woven forever into the Christian vocabulary of
prayer and devotion. They tell us of the soul's
profound hunger and thirst for God. And they tell us
also of the deep-seated need for God's supernatural
help in the supreme quest of the spiritual life, namely,
the love of God and of our fellow human beings.

(5) The psalmists have taught faith in the ultimate
triumph of righteousness. Without this, prayer would
be reduced to a rope of sand. For if we are doomed to
defeat at the start in seeking God and His righteousness, where is the glory of the quest? The psalmists
were confident that wickedness was like the "chaff
which the wind drives away." And they felt that "the
wicked will not stand in the judgment" (1:4-5). God is
holy and righteous altogether. And He alone is "from

everlasting to everlasting" (90:2). Therefore, the precepts and commandments are for all time (111:7-8). The psalmists had good reason—the only decisive reason—for their confidence in their future: They based their hopes on God's everlasting covenant of faithfulness.

The quality of a person's character and prayer-life is seen in where one turns for help in moral and spiritual matters. What is the Source? Is it work, or friends, or diversions, or a sense of humor, or gala events? One psalmist put it this way:

> I lift up my eyes to the hills.
>> From whence does my help
>> come?
> My help comes from the Lord,
>> who made heaven and earth.
> He will not let your foot be moved,
>> he who keeps you will not
>> slumber.
> Behold, he who keeps Israel
>> will neither slumber nor sleep. . . .
> The Lord will keep
>> your going out and your coming
>> in
> from this time forth and for
>> evermore. (121:1-4, 8)

Amid all the things in life that come and go, the psalmists have taught us to put our trust in the one true God whose "steadfast love and faithfulness" are "from everlasting to everlasting."

As we look toward the prophets and the New Testament, we see that the psalmists, in addition to the glory of their enduring thoughts and words, prepared the way for what Jesus and the apostles taught on prayer. The time had not come for them to leave with us that fuller teaching on prayer made possible by the revelation of God as Father, Son, and Holy Spirit. Like the prophets, they prepared the way for the Savior. And they made it easy for Christians both to use their words and to let them flow into prayers in the name of Jesus Christ. They plowed up the soil of spiritual receptivity so Christians could receive the teaching of Jesus on praying for our enemies and for each other. And they helped Christians to be open to the illuminating and empowering presence of the Holy Spirit in prayer.

WHAT JEREMIAH TAUGHT ABOUT PRAYER

Jeremiah has been called "the first man of prayer known to the history of religion" and "the father of true prayer." (See Heiler, *Prayer*, p. 122.) People have been praying since the dawn of history. Why, then, this special focus on Jeremiah? Primarily because he was the first great spiritual leader to enter into a creative, dynamic, sustained, person-to-Person prayer-life with God.

There were others who encountered such a prayer-experience sporadically and yet with some depth. Enoch walked with God. Abraham put his faith in God and entered into intercessory prayer. Moses was confronted by God and interceded for the people. As we have seen, David and the psalmists experienced moments of person-to-Person prayer as communion and encounter with God. The psalmists had already expressed in cultic and poetic form what Jeremiah experienced in his encounters with God. (On the pre-exilic origin of most of the Psalms, see Artur Weiser, *The Psalms: A Commentary*, pp. 91-95.)

With Jeremiah prayer was an overwhelming passion, sustained, intimate, personal, creative. Moreover, we have detailed knowledge of his inner life. No one can read chapters 11–20 and 23 of the book of Jeremiah without being aware of his profound experiences in the deeper dimensions of prayer.

Of what did this pioneer work consist? Three basic insights came out of Jeremiah's encounters with God in prayer.

First, Jeremiah communicated through his writings that prayer is an intimately personal conversation with God. There was a directness in this divine-human relationship that opened up new avenues of prayer for all succeeding generations. Among those who expressed the spirit of this kind of prayer were the psalmists who, along with Jeremiah, have taught those in the Judeo-Christian heritage what it means to pray.

Second, like the psalmists, Jeremiah revealed that prayer, at its best, involves us in the profoundest struggles of life. For God puts the righteous to the test (Jer. 20:12) and makes known his opposition to wickedness.

We have seen that prayer is person-to-Person communion and encounter with God. But this sounds like a pale abstraction compared to the desperate struggles of Jeremiah in his encounters with God. God met him where he was, in the heart of life, in the center of personal and community issues. The people had corrupted their religion by turning to other gods and to pagan ways. Having forgotten God's covenant, they were substituting a cheap and easy ritualism at the Temple for right living before God. Even the priests and prophets had abandoned the faith to pursue their godless ways (Jer. 23:11). Jeremiah was engaged in a continual call to repentance and to a changed heart (8:4-7; 9:5; 18:11).

Besides the internal corruption of the people and their leaders, there was the threat of domination from foreign nations. And eventually, during Jeremiah's lifetime and in keeping with his unpopular predictions, Jerusalem fell to the Babylonians. The towns of Judah were destroyed and the people were taken into captivity.

In the context of these actual and impending spiritual and political disasters, Jeremiah pours out his soul to God. Loneliness, grief, and despair come to utterance in his encounters with God. He deplores the fact that he was born and curses the day of his birth. "Woe is me, my mother, that you bore me, a man of strife and contention to the whole land!" (Jer. 15:10; 20:14-18). Overwhelmed with loneliness, he cries to God:

> I did not sit in the company of
>> merrymakers,
>> nor did I rejoice;
> I sat alone, because thy hand was
>> upon me,
>> for thou hadst filled me with
>> indignation. (15:17)

Jeremiah pours out his bitterness toward God Himself, when he prays,

> O Lord, thou hast deceived me,
>   and I was deceived;
> thou art stronger than I,
>   and thou hast prevailed.
> I have become a laughingstock all
>   the day;
>   every one mocks me. (20:7)

The word *existentialism*, widely used during the twentieth century, belongs here. It focuses on a person's inner struggles, decisions, anxieties, loneliness, alienation, doubt, despair. Jeremiah enters into the depths of existential passion in prayer. And this kind of continual trial is an inherent feature of prayer in the biblical heritage. For no one can be in the presence of God and ignore the agonizing struggles of humanity.

Third, Jeremiah taught us that no matter how dark the night, God's day is sure to come if His people will return to Him. Apart from God there is no hope. So God spoke to Jeremiah, saying:

> Cursed is the man who trusts in man
>   and makes flesh his arm,
>   whose heart turns away from the Lord. (17:5)

But the one who trusts in the Lord is like a tree that remains green and bears fruit despite the surrounding drought (17:8). The prophet's vision of God's new day comes to sublime utterance when he speaks of the glorious new covenant: "Behold, the days are coming, says the Lord, when I will make a new covenant with the house of Israel and the house of Judah. . . . I will put my law within them, and I will write it upon their hearts; and I will be their God, and they shall be my people" (31:31, 33).

Great as he was, Jeremiah left something to be desired in his prayer-life. He lacked the psalmists' sense of gratitude and thanksgiving. And he carried the spirit of vengeance too much with him when he prayed:

> Yet, thou, O Lord, knowest
>   all their plotting to slay me.
> Forgive not their iniquity,
>   nor blot out their sin from thy
>   sight. (18:23)

This is another reminder that in the biblical understanding of prayer the Old Testament prepares the way for the teaching and example of Jesus and the apostles. Much that the psalmists and prophets taught on prayer abides in its own right. Their inspired writings have ageless glory. In addition, they have the glory of preparing the way for what was yet to come.

WHAT JESUS TAUGHT ABOUT PRAYER

Before considering some specific teachings of Jesus on prayer, we need to lift up two basic facts. The first is that Jesus prayed. The second is that His example as the Man of prayer had a powerful influence on his disciples.

Jesus prayed. I am not saying that a Jewish peasant prayed, or that an unusually charismatic individual prayed. I am emphasizing the thought that Jesus

Christ, the Son of God and Savior of the world, prayed. He who is the Way, the Truth, and the Life, began and continued His mission with prayer. He commanded His followers to pray. And what He taught with His lips He demonstrated in His life (Matt. 14:23; 26:36-44; Mark 1:35; 6:46; Luke 3:21; 5:16; 6:12; 9:18, 28-29; 11:1; 22:32, 41, 44; John 17:1-26). The development of a full-orbed person-to-Person prayer-life—for which the Old Testament prepared the way—reached its highest expression in Jesus. The fact that He prayed is of utmost importance in leading us into the life of prayer. As we have seen, in the Old Testament some of the psalmists and Jeremiah attain a high level of prayer as personal communion and encounter with God. But Jesus is the Master-teacher on prayer.

What He taught about prayer is most clearly seen in the quality and influence of His example as the *Man of prayer*. The disciples of Jesus felt this profoundly. We remember that, before choosing the twelve, Jesus continued all night in prayer. Then He chose those whom He named apostles (Luke 6:12-13). Early in His ministry, the Master called them to be His helpers in His special mission in the kingdom of God. This means that they were brought into intimate personal relationships with Jesus. They ate with Him. They listened to Him. They asked Him questions within the privacy of their group. They observed Him in His work as Teacher, Physician, and Preacher. No other persons had this privilege. They alone had the first-hand knowledge of Jesus as the Man of prayer.

The disciples had seen Jesus praying. They doubtless overhead Him many times when He prayed (see Luke 11:1). They knew by direct experience that there was something different about His prayer-life from that of the Pharisees and other religious leaders. They knew that Jesus and the Heavenly Father were on the most intimate of terms. And they wanted to experience for themselves something of that same communion with the Father.

In Luke's Gospel we read the following words about Jesus: "He was praying in a certain place, and when he ceased, one of his disciples said to him, 'Lord, teach us to pray'. . . . And He said to them, 'When you pray, say:' " Then Jesus gave them Luke's version of what we call our Lord's Prayer (Luke 11:1-4). The main point here is that the twelve disciples knew not only that Jesus prayed but also that He alone could give them the guidance they needed for their own prayer-life. By His example, Jesus was for them the Master-teacher on prayer. Therefore, regarding prayer, they looked beyond the patriarchs, beyond the psalmists, and beyond the prophets to Jesus. In all of this, the apostles have guided Christians throughout the centuries. And they have taught us to look to Jesus as our final guide in our own prayer-life.

In later paragraphs, we shall consider some of the specific teachings of Jesus on how to pray. But none of those teachings can compare in importance with what our Lord has revealed through the power and inspiration of His example. And here our words seem almost helpless to tell the marvelous story of Jesus, the Man of prayer. They seem like pale abstractions compared to the unutterable glory of His life of prayer. The four Gospels tell us of the many times when He went apart to pray. They tell us of when He prayed in the hearing of a gathered multitude. They tell us of his prayers for

His disciples and for all of them who were to follow (John 17:20). And they tell us of His life—that biography of love—which moved from prayer to deeds of love and mercy.

It would not be going too far to say that, during our Lord's unique ministry on earth, His whole life might be described as an extended life of prayer. His parables and other teachings tell us of the wide ranges of His observations on the human scene. He thought of many things. He spoke of seed and soil and sowing and harvest. He reflected on mothers and fathers and children—on young and old, male and female, rich and poor, weak and strong. He knew from direct observation the peril of the love of riches. And, by virtue of His continuing experiences with both friends and enemies, He knew what was in human beings. In the thick of life in community, He carried out His mission. He laughed and wept. He healed the sick. He preached and taught. And He suffered and died for the sins of the world.

Somehow, amid all of his many thoughts, observations, and deeds, everything He did seems to have flowed from Him as the supreme Man of prayer. And when we behold Him on the Cross, we know that what happened there came out of His prayer in that garden of agony. Out of His prayer at Gethsemane, everything was transmuted until an otherwise obscure garden became a hallowed spot in Christian history because of the Master's supreme moment of prayer in that place. It was there more than anywhere else that Jesus taught us to put our absolute trust in God even in the midst of our most desperate circumstances. His triumph in prayer at Gethsemane and Calvary teaches us that God's redemptive mission throughout the whole world must go on at all cost. Jesus had His cross to bear, and, as we pray and work in the kingdom, we know that we too must deny ourselves and take up our cross and follow Him.

Jesus taught us the unutterable beauty and glory of a life of prayer which issues in deeds of sheer courage and total dedication to God. He demonstrated what can happen when we return again and again to the Father in prayer until all else that we do receives its motivation and power from God.

By example, as well as precept, Jesus taught us also that His own prayer life came from His understanding of God and human beings. It is beyond question that Jesus' approach to prayer was based on His understanding of God as Father. If we think of God merely as a Cosmic Process, we cannot enter into a person-to-Person prayer-life. We cannot pray to a process, whether cosmic or not. If we believe that God is a vague impersonal Being-in-itself, prayer is almost sure to be reduced to meditation and aspiration. But, with Jesus, God *is* Father. God is personal. He knows us, loves us, cares for us, and responds to us. So, inevitably, there is with Jesus this sense of the most intimate interpersonal relationship with God. This is doubtless one reason why He deliberately taught His disciples to begin their prayer with the words, "Our Father." Yet Jesus did not in the least reduce the sense of the greatness and glory of God. Therefore, He taught his disciples to pray:

> Our Father, who art in heaven,
> Hallowed be Thy name.

Jesus was the only founder of a world religion to teach his followers to pray to God as Father. He was not teaching them to think of God in terms of maleness. For he knew God to be a Spirit who is neither male nor female. We may throw some light on this matter of God and sexuality by two brief comments. The first is that there is in the English language no pronoun which transcends or rises above the male and female genders. To speak of God as "it" would be to reduce Him to an impersonal term which is repugnant to the biblical revelation. The second comment is that we get the best insight into who God is through what we experience as our own personhood, or mind, or soul. To use the last term, our souls are neither male nor female. And the qualities which define our nature as souls are those which enable us to gain some understanding of the personal God revealed in the Bible. To be sure, the qualities whereby we identify ourselves (consciousness, selfhood, self-identity, knowledge, purpose, volition, love, the power to communicate, *et cetera*) are finite and radically limited. But they provide the best clues we have to understanding the personal God in whom Jesus taught us to believe. And these categories are neither male nor female. Therefore, when we use the words "He" or "Him" or "His"—with the capital H—the clear purpose is to go beyond any thought of maleness in contrast to femaleness. The category of sex has no assignable meaning in relation to God.

The combination of the infinite greatness of God and His marvelous approachability guided the disciples of Jesus in their prayer-life. And the understanding of God as Father has informed the prayers of the continuing community of faith throughout the centuries. So we pray to God as Father. And though prayer is a dynamic source of creative energy, it is always communion and encounter with God. It is both an end-in-itself and a divinely appointed means of doing God's work.

What did Jesus teach about how to pray? He taught at least seven things.

First he taught us to be brief,* to come to the point and to be specific. He taught us to pray for forgiveness and for the power to carry out God's holy purpose. He taught us also to pray for daily bread and for victory over temptation. Physical and spiritual needs were joined together with sublime brevity in our Lord's Prayer. The effect of this teaching is to keep us away from pompous, ostentatious, and unnatural language in prayer. "And in praying do not heap up empty phrases as the Gentiles do; for they think that they will be heard for their many words" (Matt. 6:7).

Second, Jesus taught us to pray in faith and to expect results. He said, "Ask, and it will be given you; seek, and you will find; knock, and it will be opened to you" (Matt. 7:7). When He said, "Ask," He did not mean "make a casual request." When He said, "Seek," He did not mean "look around a little." And when He said, "Knock," He did not mean "tap on the door lightly." The words *ask, seek,* and *knock* are strong words. They suggest that in prayer we must be bold, passionate, and earnest. They suggest also that we must pray in faith, knowing that God wants to bless us. For, as Jesus said, "If you then, who are evil, know how to give good gifts to your children, how

---

*This was the general rule. But we know, of course, that at times Jesus could not be brief because he continued all night in prayer for special purposes. And in the Garden of Gethsemane, He agonized in prayer far longer than a few brief moments.

much more will your Father who is in heaven give good things to those who ask him!" (Matt. 7:11-12; Luke 11:13; see also Matt. 17:14-21; 21:21-22; Mark 11:20-24; Luke 11:5-9; John 16:24). The words "how much more" are crucial. An imperfect parent wants to do good things for the children. *How much more* does the Father who is perfect and holy want to bless His children! Therefore, we are to pray in faith and expect God's blessings.

Third, Jesus taught us to be persistent in prayer. This thought builds on the preceding one. Here the mind of the Master meets the best insights of psychology by weaving into the life of prayer the principle of a sustained desire. God responds graciously to those who, in keeping with His purpose, let their desires come to focus in their prayers. This promise of blessings is particularly true of those who hunger and thirst for righteousness, for "they shall be satisfied" (Matt. 5:6). And those who seek first the kingdom of God and His righteousness will receive many other blessings (Matt. 6:33). Prayer and losing heart do not mix. The Master illustrated this graphically in his parable of the widow's persistence before the unrighteous judge (Luke 18:1-8).

Fourth, Jesus taught that basic honesty is an indispensable condition for true prayer. He wanted us to be honest enough not to hide our sins and frailties under a mask of forms and ceremonies. So he said, "If you abide in me, and my words abide in you, ask whatever you will, and it shall be done for you. By this my Father is glorified, that you bear much fruit, and so prove to be my disciples" (John 15:7-8). The parable of the Pharisee and the publican illustrates this (Luke 18:9-14). The Master knew that everyone could be aware of a basic rightness or wrongness with God. And He knew that the only way to approach the Father is in the spirit of honesty, sincerity, and consequently the willingness to obey. This is why Jesus taught his followers to pray in His name (John 14:13, 14; 15:16; 16:23, 24, 26). For when we pray in the name of Jesus, we are filled with His spirit and seek what He wants. In this way our prayers will rise to God out of the inward flow of the love of Christ.

Fifth, Jesus taught His followers to pray for each other and for the needs of the whole world. This is seen in His call to pray "the Lord of the harvest to send out laborers into his harvest" (Matt. 9:35-39). This spirit of intercession is implied also in the Master's repeated instructions on forgiving others "so that your Father also who is in heaven may forgive you your trespasses" (Mark 11:25). Through prayer and fasting we can do great things for others (Matt. 17:19-21). The powers of evil, both within and without, are often defeated by the earnest prayers of the faithful.

Jesus prayed for Peter, that he might be delivered from the power of Satan. He said, "Simon, Simon, behold, Satan demanded to have you, that he might sift you like wheat, but I have prayed for you that your faith may not fail; and when you have turned again, strengthen your brethren" (Luke 22:31-32). All of the Master's teaching on praying for others was brought to a magnificent summation in His own great prayer for His followers (John, chapter 17). He carried this further when He included us too. For He said, "I do not pray for these only, but also for those who are to believe in me through their word, that they may all be one . . ." (John 17:20-21). We may have our doubts about praying for others, but Jesus did not. Christians throughout the centuries have practiced the habit of praying for others, and God has blessed them with abundant harvests.

Sixth, Jesus taught us to express thanksgiving in prayer. When the seventy returned with joy from their mission as evangels, Jesus prayed: " 'I thank thee, Father, Lord of heaven and earth, that thou hast hidden these things from the wise and understanding and revealed them to babes; yea, Father, for such was thy gracious will' " (Luke 10:21). And before the tomb of Lazarus He prayed: "Father, I thank thee that thou hast heard me" (John 11:41). It was no accident that Paul, who determined to imitate Jesus (I Cor. 11:1), became the great champion of gratitude as an essential characteristic of the Christian. Through Jesus the practice of being thankful to God became a basic principle of the devotional life.

Seventh, Jesus taught that the supreme purpose of prayer is to glorify God and to strive with Him in the work of the kingdom. We cannot emphasize too much the Father's holy purpose for all His children. God wants us to respond to His love, to receive His grace and blessings, and to weave into our passing earthly lives His holy concerns. In this Jesus was our perfect example. He made it His habit to go apart for prayer before His major decisions. Before entering upon his public ministry, He went into the wilderness to pray (Matt. 4:1-11; Mark 1:12-13; Luke 4:1-13). He went out to a mountain to pray—and continued all night in prayer—before making his final selection of the twelve disciples from among his followers (Luke 6:12-16).

The greatest sentence ever uttered in a prayer is this:

> Thy kingdom come,
> Thy will be done,
>   On earth as it is in heaven. (Matt. 6:10)

For if we do not pray this prayer, we need not pray any other. It is the foundation on which all Christian prayers are built. Jesus demonstrated His commitment to God's holy purpose during His agonizing prayer at Gethsemane when He said, ". . . nevertheless not my will, but thine, be done" (Luke 22:42).

As the Master-teacher in the life of prayer, Jesus Christ abides through all generations. For in this too He is "the same yesterday and today and for ever" (Heb. 13:8). There are huge gala spectacles throughout the world where vast multitudes come together to hear popular music, to witness athletic events, and to participate in political conventions. In the light of these and the countless other distractions which capture the people's attention, we sometimes feel that Jesus Christ and His call to prayer are lost in the tumult and the shouting.

But long after these spectacles and diversions have tumbled down the currents of history and flowed into the vast ocean of oblivion, the imperial glory of the life of Christ will continue to capture young people everywhere and command the allegiance of people of all ages. His mighty act of redemption on the cross abides forever. And His life of prayer will guide people throughout the world as they choose to join each other in the ageless pilgrimage with God.

WHAT PAUL TAUGHT ABOUT PRAYER

Next to Jesus, Paul was the greatest teacher on prayer that the world has seen. He taught the congregations he formed to be praying communities—so much so, in fact, that he has been called the creator of Christian congregational prayer. He helped people to avoid the pitfalls of an artificial prayer-life by emphasizing the permanent, sustaining factors in authentic prayer.

What are those emphases, which Paul taught by precept and example, that have guided the community of prayer, faith, and service throughout the centuries? Paul shared with us four things that have a permanent place in the Christian practice of prayer.

First, he taught that our fellowship with God is directly related to the centrality of Jesus Christ. There is a curious mixture of mystery and insight here. We do not know in human terms why it is that somehow when we meditate on Jesus Christ, think of what He said and did, and decide to follow Him, we feel ourselves mysteriously drawn to God. We only know it is so. But this is not merely a human discovery: It is a divine revelation. Our communion with God through Jesus Christ moves from the more mystical and abstract sense of the divine Presence toward the intimately personal awareness of the loving Father.

In Paul this Christ-centeredness in prayer was inevitable because his new life as a whole revolved around Jesus Christ. He did not find in his Hebrew heritage what he most wanted. To be sure, he was inspired by Abraham, Moses, the prophets and the psalmists. But he understood them to be chosen by God to prepare the way for moving from the law to grace. So his supreme source of the new life came from Christ.

How did it happen that this Pharisee of the Pharisees (who was determined to outrun his peers) should focus on Jesus Christ as the supreme source of spiritual power? Perhaps he saw a level of spiritual victory in the Christians whom he had been persecuting. And surely he saw this in Stephen, who prayed for those who were killing him. So Saul, this determined, persistent, spiritual athlete, now saw a new realm of possibility for his soul. Then followed the awful inner conflict which was mercifully resolved when the Risen Lord confronted him on the road to Damascus. Therefore, when Paul talked, preached, or wrote about prayer, it was Christ-centered. For through Christ alone he knew himself to be a "new creation." Through Christ he was lifted into the new dimension of existence as a Christian.

No wonder he spoke of Jesus as "the power of God and the wisdom of God" (I Cor. 1:24). Paul "decided to know nothing among you except Jesus Christ and him crucified" (I Cor. 2:2). He declared: "I have been crucified with Christ; it is no longer I who live, but Christ who lives in me . . ." (Gal. 2:20).

It is not surprising that the man who spoke thus out of the deepest recesses of his own spirituality should have made Christ central in his prayer-life. When he thanked God, he did so "through Jesus Christ" (Rom. 1:8). When he asked others to give thanks in all circumstances it was because "this is the will of God in Christ Jesus for you" (I Thess. 5:18). Paul remembered the Christians at Ephesus in his prayers and prayed that "the God of our Lord Jesus Christ, the Father of glory," might give them a spirit of wisdom and of revelation in the knowledge of Christ (Eph. 1:16-17). It is almost impossible to exaggerate the creative power of Christ in the prayer-life of Paul. Everything centers in Christ. Everything flows from God through Him. And in prayer the divine grace transforms through Christ.

This brings us to the second major emphasis Paul made in his teaching on prayer. He, more than anyone else except Jesus, insisted that gratitude or thanksgiving is essential in all true Christian prayer. Indeed, for Paul gratitude to God was a permanent feature of a healthy Christian life. And in prayer thanksgiving was poured out to God as an essential feature of the devout life.

As we have seen, Paul said that we should give thanks in all circumstances. This means that in sickness or health, in tragedy or triumph, in sorrow or joy, we should give thanks to God. Then, as if to show that this is no merely whimsical utterance, he said that we should do this because it is "the will of God in Christ Jesus" (I Thess. 5:18). Nothing here suggests that we should be thankful *for* bad circumstances. Rather, we should be thankful *in* all circumstances.

Paul gave thanks to God when he wrote to the Christians in Rome because their faith was "proclaimed in all the world" (Rom. 1:8). He was filled with gratitude because of the supernatural deliverance from sin: "Thanks be to God through Jesus Christ our Lord!" (Rom. 7:25). He urged the Ephesians to "be filled with the Spirit, addressing one another in psalms and hymns and spiritual songs, singing and making melody to the Lord with all your heart, always and for everything giving thanks in the name of our Lord Jesus Christ to God the Father"

(Eph. 5:18-20). In his prayers for the Philippians, Paul expressed his gratitude to God for their "partnership in the gospel" (Phil. 1:3-5). He urged them to "rejoice in the Lord" (3:1) and to make their prayer and supplication with thanksgiving (4:6). Again and again, by precept and example, Paul called upon the Christians to rejoice and give thanks in their prayers (I Thess. 1:2; 2:13; 5:16-18; Phil. 4:6).

Paul brought to the understanding of prayer a third major emphasis which has a permanent place in Christian prayer. Just as Paul guided the early Christian congregations in expressing gratitude, so Paul shaped the church's mind on intercessory prayer. He practiced it and taught it with a passion. As Heiler says, "Paul has put intercessory prayer at the very centre of the devotional life of the Christian. He himself, the great missionary and pastor, was a master of the art of intercessory prayer" (*Prayer*, p. 124).

Paul prayed indefatigably for the people in the churches he established. And to those in Rome—whose church he did not establish—he wrote: "For God is my witness . . . that without ceasing I mention you always in my prayers . . ." (Rom. 1:9). He prayed continuously for the christians at Corinth (I Cor. 1:4-8; II Cor. 13:7-9), for those at Ephesus (Eph. 1:15-17), for those at Philippi (Phil. 1:3-5), and for those at Thessalonica (I Thess. 1:2-3). He prayed for individuals like Philemon, Apphia, and Archippus (Philemon 2-4).

And of course in addition he asked other Christians to pray for him as they prayed for each other. For despite all of his extraordinary experiences and abilities he felt profoundly the need for the prayers of

Christians in the churches (Rom. 15:30-32; II Cor. 1:11; Phil. 1:19-20; Col. 4:3; I Thess. 5:25).

One more emphasis which Paul brought in his teaching on prayer is that of constancy. No merely sporadic efforts will be adequate to the need. There is doubtless a place for those sudden ventures into prayer which come out of the depths of tragedy. But, as Paul saw, these are not normative in Christian experience. So he invited people to be constant in prayer and thus to practice prayer as a habit of Christian living. He said to the Romans, "Rejoice in your hope, be patient in tribulation, be constant in prayer" (Rom. 12:12). He asked the Ephesians to "pray at all times in the Spirit" (Eph. 6:18). He urged the Thessalonians to "pray constantly" (I Thess. 5:17). And he enjoined the Colossians to "continue steadfastly in prayer, being watchful in it with thanksgiving" (Col. 4:2-3).

We hear much these days about life-styles. Even the Christian life has been called a life-style. This suggests that Christianity is just a fashion among other ways of living. This kind of thinking is far removed from Paul's understanding of what it means to be a Christian. To Paul, steadfastness in prayer was a life-principle and not a life-style. For a Christian is a person of prayer and faith who, not conforming to the paltry standards of this world, lives under the sway of Jesus Christ.

CHAPTER THREE

Prayer and Some Basic Problems

PRAYER AND OUR THOUGHTS

It is easy to see obvious mistakes. Everyone knows when a baseball player makes an error. Everyone can see when a juggler misses the act. And everyone knows the obvious enemies of God and prayer. We do not require special instruction to see that alcoholism, drug addiction, lying, stealing, cursing, greed, lust, disloyalty, and violence shut out God and prayer.

But many things take place within us which are almost too close to see. I have in mind the everflowing streams of consciousness with their movements from thought to thought and experience to experience. During every waking moment we are thinking of something. And often in our sleep things flow into our minds apparently without much rhyme or reason. Most of our thoughts, day or night, come in and pass away. They are soon lost in the vast oblivion of forgotten things. This stream of consciousness in each of us—which continues to flow through an abiding self—is characteristic of our human nature. To ask people to stop this flow is to invite them to stop living.

Therefore, the walk with God, the practice of prayer, must take place within souls which experience this continual inner flow of thoughts.

In the light of this bedrock fact about ourselves, we can understand the significance of the extensive efforts toward thought-control, self-understanding, and disciplined living. Socrates gave the world something important when he said, "Know thyself." Jesus made statements of supreme importance on how to save our souls by losing them in devotion to God and others. These and countless other teachings and maxims concern the organization and control of our thoughts. Therefore they have an ageless relevance.

Who are we? What goes into our makeup? At least three things: thoughts, desires, and emotions. And these are mysteriously interwoven to form strangely diverse patterns. Sometimes, in our most lucid moments, we seem to think clearly. When we have to make practical decisions, our thinking gets focused and it directs our actions. But much of the time there is no such clarity and focus.

Consider now our thoughts. By a thought I mean whatever is an object of attention. And, when we stop long enough to see what is going on, we realize how fleeting our attention span is. There are all sorts of thoughts, and these are related to our bodies. Our thoughts are not our brains and nervous systems. But, in this present life, they are dependent on our brains, nervous systems, and bodily organs.* How

---

*This fact has led some scientists and others to hold that even our thoughts are physical. But this does not follow. The confusion results from supposing that because our thoughts have a *causal basis* in our brains and nervous systems, they *are* those physical things. But a thought is a thought and not a part of the brain, not a process of the brain, and not anything other than what it presents itself as being.

this is possible is a mystery. Just because something is a mystery does not make it unreal. Life is a mystery, but we live it.

Again, all of our thoughts have a basis in our physical bodies. And some of our thoughts are determined by our physical condition. For example, if we have a headache, we move from other thoughts to the medicine cabinet. Hunger puts thoughts of food into our minds. So we head for the refrigerator. Disorders of body lead to disorders in thoughts. Mental disarrangements—in which people cannot distinguish between imagination and reality—arise in no small degree from physical disarrangements.

But it is self-evident that our normal thoughts are directly connected with our bodies. For example, we *see* other people and greet them. We *hear* their words and converse with them. We *smell* various odors, we *touch* knives and forks, and we *taste* foods. Our thoughts in daily life flow extensively from our senses. All of this is an inherent, God-ordained reality of human life on earth. Therefore, nothing that is said about prayer and our thoughts is an invitation or hint that we should stop using our organs of sense.

Our thoughts, like our dreams, often arise from half-forgotten experiences that lie sleeping in our subconscious processes. What this tells us is that we should let our conscious moments feed our subconscious processes with good things. And this pattern is in harmony with a creative prayer-life.

In addition, we cannot help having all sorts of *associations of ideas.* One thought suggests another by a natural process. For many years the psychologists have been writing on the law of the association of ideas. Long before the psychologists, great novelists and dramatists have shown how the minds of human beings function by means of this law. And we would find it hard to make our way through any day of practical living without the power of our minds to make these connections. We see a neighbor, and various thoughts naturally arise in association with the one we see. Space relations, time relations, and interpersonal relations are all made possible by this law. Therefore, in prayer we do not trample upon this God-ordained mental process. We use it.

Now turn with me to certain types of thoughts which obstruct the way to a vital prayer-life. Consider three such types of thought: (1) reverie, (2) idle curiosity, and (3) thoughts which arise from destructive emotions.

Reverie. Reverie is a free flow of thoughts which are largely disconnected from our real situation. For example, sometimes when we are listening to a lecture or a sermon, our minds drift off into far-away thoughts. Reverie is the opposite of concentration. It is distraction of mind. And often it is building castles in the air, or entertaining fanciful hopes. Frequently, our reveries revolve around our beloved egos. For our self-love is like the restless sea. Our thoughts return again and again to fanciful games of self-justification. Our reveries may take us up to the high plateau of a fool's paradise or plunge us into the depths of a coward's hell.

In a memorable expression of honesty, the poet-clergyman John Donne (1573–1631) tells of what may take place even in a saintly soul in prayer.

I throw myself down in my chamber and call in and invite God and His angels thither, and when they are there I neglect God and His angels for the noise of a fly, for the rattling of a coach, for the whining of a door. I talk on in the same posture of praying, eyes lifted up, knees bowed down, as though I prayed to God, and if God or His angels should ask me when I thought last of God in that prayer, I cannot tell. Sometimes I find that I had forgot what I was about, but when I began to forget it I cannot tell. A memory of yesterday's pleasures, a fear of tomorrow's dangers, a straw under my knee, a noise in mine ear, a light in mine eye, an anything, a nothing, a fancy, a chimera in my brain troubles me in my prayer.

Reverie is a universal problem in our prayer-life. In prayer we seek the "power from on high." In reverie there is no power. To be sure, there are times when we need to let our minds graze in the beautiful pastures of fantasy. But prayer is serious business. For we are in the presence of God, kneeling in awe and reverence, and opening our souls to Him. In true prayer we experience godly sorrow for our sins and we express our sincere desire to obey God and serve Him. We pray for the grace to be forgiven and the willingness to forgive any who misunderstand or mistreat us. We pray for the power to conquer temptation. And we yearn for the Holy Spirit to fill our souls with the love of God and neighbor.

What is the answer to this universal tendency to be drawn away from God by our reveries? The answer takes us to the heart-principle of the devotional life, namely, *in returning shall be your strength* (see Isa. 30:15). We cannot think of God all the time. When driving our cars, we have to look at the road, take in the traffic situation, observe the signs, know when to stop and go. When buying groceries, we have to observe the quality of the fruits and vegetables, and make judgments on what else to buy. So is it all along the way each day. Therefore, we must set aside times daily when we return to God and the things of God. This is the significance of regular times for public worship and Bible study.

It is this habit that gives meaning to Paul's call to pray without ceasing (I Thess. 5:17; Rom. 12:12). For when we return to God at planned intervals, all else that we do is pervaded with the mysterious sense of the presence of God.

Idle curiosity. Anything which tends to trivialize our relationships with others is an enemy of prayer in the biblical heritage. Idle curiosity usually concerns our thoughts about other people. And frequently it sinks to the level of cheap gossip. We are all aware that there is a worthy place for human interest in one another. Our curiosity may arise from a sincere human interest which leads to giving the cup of cold water to the thirsty or housing to the homeless. But what I have in mind here are trains of thoughts disconnected from any desire to act in behalf of others. Sometimes these thoughts drift harmlessly into our minds and quickly pass away. Two people at a dinner table in a restaurant are whispering. What about? Another person is reading a letter intently. What is in it? Someone gets up in the middle of a sermon and walks out of the church. Why? Such idle curiosity is distracting, but, except for the waste of time and energy, it is relatively harmless.

Turn this around and look at the other side of it. Often idle curiosity, like a dreadful plague, leads us to say things about others which hurt or destroy them. The magazines devoted to gossip thrive on this universal idle curiosity. Their editors know where their market is. They know that scandal and oddity need no supporting argument. Even in church circles scandal may be played up again and again until we feel like crying out: Cease! Have done with lesser things! Press forward for the glory of God and the blessings for our fellow human beings!

One of the most notable differences between one human being and another is seen in their powers of concentration. Some people make up their minds what they want to do, and they do it. They refuse to waste time and energy on day-dreams, distractions, and idle curiosity. Others live on the misty flats where their thoughts drift to and fro. When we pray, we hear God's call to the serious business of being disciples of Jesus Christ.

Here again we find the answer in the heart-principle of the devotional life: In returning shall be your strength.

Thoughts that arise from destructive emotions. By destructive emotions I mean those feelings and attitudes that strike against our eternal happiness. John Wesley wrote one of his most interesting sermons on "Wandering Thoughts" (*Works,* vol. 2, sermon 41). There he distinguishes between those thoughts that are sinful and those that are not. He says:

> Again: all thoughts which spring from sinful tempers are undoubtedly sinful. Such, for instance, are those that spring from a revengeful temper, from pride, or lust, or vanity. "An evil tree cannot bring forth good fruit," therefore if the tree be evil, so must the fruit be also.

And so must those be which either produce or feed any sinful temper; those which either give rise to pride or vanity, to anger or love of the world, or confirm and increase these or any other unholy temper, passion, or affection. For not only whatever flows from evil is evil, but also whatever leads to it; whatever tends to alienate the soul from God, and to make or keep it "earthly, sensual, and devilish." (*Works*, vol. 2, p. 132)

All of us know what pride is: it is inordinate self-love. It is thinking of ourselves more highly than we ought (Rom. 12:3). This turns our thoughts away from God's purpose for us, makes us deaf even to constructive criticism, and leads us into a fatal complacency. Hatred leads to resentment, which is sustained hostility. This in turn leads to vengeance. And all of these, whether taken in small doses or large, are poison. Think of all the evil thoughts that arise from hatred! Because of these, Jesus emphasized his teaching on loving our enemies (Matt. 5:44; 6:12). And Paul, in imitating Jesus, says, "Beloved, never avenge yourselves, but leave it to the wrath of God" (Rom. 12:19).

Lust produces thoughts of adultery, abnormal sexual practices, and betrayal. Greed leads to numberless evil thoughts and inhuman actions. Money is important, but, as the Bible teaches concerning the economic realm, "The love of money is the root of all evils" (I Tim. 6:10). And think of all the destructive thoughts awakened in our minds by despair! Some of them come to expression in the following words: Why me? What am I to do? What can I do? Poor-little-me. Everybody is against me. Nobody understands me. What will become of me?

By a bad spirit I mean a chronically negative attitude. At this point, a word of caution is needed. Let us remember that we do not sin when evil thoughts merely flow into our consciousness. Jesus himself experienced clearly what Satan meant by his temptations. But he did not thereby sin. All kinds of thoughts may come and go without our yielding to them. We become sinners when we nurture evil thoughts and let them have room and board in the habitation of our souls.

The only answer to all evil thoughts that arise from our destructive emotions is to pray earnestly for God, by his grace, to cure those emotions. They are to be driven out by the power of God in Jesus Christ. This inner transformation has been called the expulsive power of a great affection. It is made possible through prayer, by which we become completely open to receive the love of Christ. And if this love of God in Christ is to be sustained against all the assaults of the enemy, we must follow the grand heart-principle of the devotional life: In returning shall be your strength.

PRAYER AND THAT ONE MAJOR DEFECT

A combination of qualities is necessary to succeed in anything. In athletics, in addition to superior physical talents, a person needs determination, concentration, temperate habits, and the desire to win. In business, education, law, labor, farming, and daily work of any kind, many qualities are necessary for success.

Being a Christian also requires a combination of virtues such as faith, hope, love, and wisdom. But, by a strange twist, all we need is one major defect to put a blight upon our character and witness. That defect may put us under such a burden of guilt as to snuff out the inner witness. It may lead to doubts and fears which shut the door to faith. It will stand in the way of spiritual growth. And it often leads us into cheap excuses and tricky efforts to justify ourselves.

Moreover, any major defect will surely mar our Christian witness. Most basic of all is the inner damage done to our souls by a major defect. For, as Jesus said, a house divided against itself cannot stand (Mark 3:25). In the end such a defect shuts one out of the kingdom of God.

There is a remarkable episode in Shakespeare's *Hamlet* in which Hamlet is looking down on a scene of drunkenness and revelry. He reflects on what he sees and observes that this is the problem of his people as a nation. The whole world judges them by this folly. Then he applies this to the individual as follows:

> So, oft it chances in particular men,
> That for some vicious mole of nature in them,
> As, in their birth—wherein they are not guilty,
> Since nature cannot choose his origin—
> By the o'ergrowth of some complexion,
> Oft breaking down the pales and forts of reason,
> Or by some habit that too much o'er-leavens
> The form of plausive manners, that these men—
> Carrying, I say, the stamp of one defect,
> Being nature's livery, or fortune's star—
> Their virtues else—be they as pure as grace,
> As infinite as man may undergo—
> Shall in the general censure take corruption
> From that particular fault. . . .
> (*Hamlet*, I, 4)

At this point I can almost hear someone say: "But surely a Christian does not have any such major defect." I understand this, but I have to recognize the plain fact of our imperfections. At the same time I want us to hear the Master's call to move toward perfection. Wesley preached on "Sin in Believers" (*Works*, Vol. 1, Sermon 13). At the outset Wesley reminded his hearers that since ancient times Christians have warned themselves of the continuing warfare between the "flesh" and the "spirit." Even after we have been forgiven, we are apt to falter and to fail the Savior who summons us to righteousness. The words of Paul on this were written to believers (Gal. 5:17; I Cor. 3:1-3). Wesley pointed out that even though we are "new creations" (II Cor. 5:17), we still may not have "the whole mind which was in Christ" (Sermon 13, p. 326).

What defect so mars the life of the Christian as to reduce his or her effectiveness and witness? For one person it will be one thing and for another something else. It might be anger which hardens into bitterness. It might be some habit—like alcoholism or drug addiction—which maintains a ruffian grip on a person who is struggling to become a Christian. Or it might be needless ignorance. We are all ignorant, but there is such a thing as unnecessary ignorance. It may be that our defect is that we are too easily hurt.

That one defect may be an uncontrolled tongue which spews out venom in anger or assassinates a character in gossip. Or it might even be the perfectionist tendency, according to which a person is overdemanding both of himself and of others. Everything has to be just right. Everything must be on time, in place, and in line. There is value in this—and certainly we ought to be on time whenever possible—but we require some give and take in dealing with each other. The understanding heart is far more important than the perfectionist tendency—and it comes much closer to Christian perfection.

Once more, that one defect may be that we believe in Christ but do not believe in the church. This is an error both of the head and the heart. For there never has been, is not now, and cannot be any sustained expression of God's good news in Christ apart from a community of believers. Without a community of faith, Christian experience and witness are reduced to fitful occasions of enthusiasm and fleeting moments of history. Isolated Christians do not last long, and they are apt to have little or no influence in the world. For this reason, in the Old Testament, God worked through the people of Israel. And, in the New Testament, while there is always the Master's concern for each person, there is also His concern to form the disciples into a body of believers. In addition, we can never forget that He came preaching the gospel of the *kingdom* of God.

Everyone can know what his or her major defect is. It may be something other than anything mentioned in the foregoing paragraphs. But whatever that one defect may be, there is the promise of victory over it by the grace of God.

Many people think that the best answer is to be found in resolutions. We resolve to overcome that one defect. But the Bible does not give much basis for hope in our human resolutions. To be sure, it may be helpful to make a resolution to indicate our determination to gain the mastery of a defect. But much more is needed. So in the Bible we hear God's call to reach beyond our human efforts and to enter the realm of earnest prayer.

Resolutions are apt to be fitful and spasmodic. True prayer is persistent and sustained. Resolutions often lack seriousness. Prayer is serious business with God. Above all, resolutions tend to leave God out. Prayer brings God in.

What we require, in order to come to grips with some really basic defect, is all the help we can get from God as well as from ourselves and others. Many times a person feels as though he or she were going down for the third time. The yearning for victory is often desperate. God, in His infinite love and wisdom, has provided the way to victory over that one defect, namely, through earnest sustained prayer. And when this passionate personal prayer is combined with the intercessory prayers and supportive fellowship within the community of faith, there are vast resources available from God for giving us the help we need.

When we pray for God to help us, we need to be specific. We need to focus on that one defect—known to us, to those who love us most, and to God—and pray for divine help for victory over it *just for today.* And when we do, in full earnestness and faith, God will give us the victory. His grace is sufficient for us in all circumstances (II Cor. 12:9). And numberless Christians throughout the centuries have told the great story of how God has given them the victory through Jesus Christ.

Paul, of course, is our master spokesman on the life-changing power of God through Jesus Christ. In one of his finest moments of inspiration, he says, ". . . but I see in my members another law at war with the law of my mind and making me captive to the law of sin which dwells in my members. Wretched man that I am! Who will deliver me from this body of death? Thanks be to God through Jesus Christ our Lord!" (Rom. 7:23-25).

Then Paul goes on to say, "There is therefore now no condemnation for those who are in Christ Jesus. For the law of the Spirit of life in Christ Jesus has set me free from the law of sin and death" (Rom. 8:1-2). Another inspired writer confirms all this when he says, "For whatever is born of God overcomes the world; and this is the victory that overcomes the world, our faith (I John 5:4).

Above all, we need to understand that every major defect is against God and others and ourselves. Therefore, beyond any particular defect, we need to pray for such a floodtide of love for God, and for others, and for ourselves that any soul-threatening, life-destroying defect will be washed away by divine grace. Here our prayers will be aimed toward that inward holiness which leads to outward holiness. This inward holiness is the love of God with all our heart, soul, mind, and strength, and the love of neighbor as ourselves. This kind of love comes only by grace through faith. It is of utmost importance to believe, in the name of Jesus, that this prayer will be answered (John 16:24).

Christian history, since the days of the apostles, bears witness to this empowering grace of Jesus Christ. And this includes the power over any soul-threatening defect in our moral and spiritual life. For Christ came to set us free from what holds us in bondage. Nothing can convince me that there is any such defect in our character from which we cannot be delivered with the help of Almighty God. But we must do our part. We must realize with godly sorrow the seriousness of whatever drags us down and separates us from God. And we must pray and strive passionately and persistently for God's deliverance. Then the promised help is on its way to make us more than conquerors through Jesus Christ our Lord.

PRAYER AND OUR FEARS

Everyone knows what fear is. It is a basic uneasiness about the past, present, or future. It is that "common quaking in the breast" which we all feel when we have lost something or are about to lose something that is precious to us: a dear one, life, health, reputation, property, liberty. More often than not, our fears focus on the future: What is going to happen to us? What is to become of us? These are the key questions.

There are fears that are rooted in reality. But many of them are imaginary. They have little or no basis in the real world. We see a small cloud and imagine a storm. We see a drop of blood and suspect a murder. We expect the worst and dread it. We take a little balloon shaped like a lion and blow it up into a monster.

Where our fears are concerned our imagination plays havoc with us. Today we are constantly led to exaggerate the dangers because of the numberless news reports on threatening events. Murder, robbery, drug addiction, alcoholism, rape, and even wrong living unpunished by the law alarm us. Nuclear destruction, pollution, overpopulation, starvation, and death stalk about before us like giants.

"Fear hath more devils than vast hell can hold." But whether imagined or real, fear incapacitates us for effective living.

Every Christian knows this destructive power of fear and, with God's help, finds a creative response to it. Every Christian who practices the life of prayer has discovered how best to handle fear.

When we pray we become calm. Anxiety gradually slips away and simple faith emerges. We begin to think about things as they are. Our imagination, once running wild, gives way to sober thought. We take our eyes off ourselves and turn them toward God and others. Moreover, in prayer we think of Jesus and His courage in facing the most awesome opposition and suffering. Courage breeds courage. In prayer also the Christian is likely to call to mind some of the great verses of the Bible. Many of these verses came out of the never-ending encounters with fear. They spoke to the needs of those who went before us, and they speak to our needs. In addition, we can receive renewed courage by reading or singing some of the great hymns of the Church. And we find wonderful mysterious spiritual resources for conquering fear in the fellowship of believers.

We turn now to the most important reason why prayer conquers fear. *When we pray we are looking to the One who alone is greater than the sum total of all our fears.* The only final answer to fear must be found in resources that are more powerful than fear. These flow into our souls from God through faith. And faith means putting our trust in God no matter what happens. The great characters of the Bible conquered fear by turning from themselves to God. They found the answer in God, before whom all our fears are defeated. For God graciously acts to free us from the bondage to fears. The psalmist said, "I will fear no evil." Why? Because he could say also: "For thou art with me." Isaiah experienced this great resource when God said to him:

> Fear not, for I am with you,
>   be not dismayed, for I am your
>   God;
> I will strengthen you, I will help
>   you,
>   I will uphold you with my
>   victorious right hand.
> (Isaiah 41:10)

And when we experience the presence of the living Christ, we know that He "charms our fears" and "sets the prisoner free."

Paul not only asked, "Who shall separate us from the love of Christ?" He specified the enemies which threaten us. "Shall tribulation, or distress, or persecution, or famine, or nakedness, or peril, or sword?" Then he who had experienced these evils added, "No, in all these things we are more than conquerors through him who loved us" (Rom. 8:35-37).

Further still, when we pray in preparation for daily living, we find our souls purified. Dishonesty in dealing with others, however subtle, is a major source of fear. Tell a lie and you have to remember what you said. Dishonesty in interpersonal relations breeds lies upon lies and consequently fears upon fears.

> The wicked flee when no one pursues,
> but the righteous are bold as a lion. (Proverb 28:1)

Prayer cleanses the soul and sets it free from those subtle forms of deception which are seedbeds of fear. For this reason prayer conquers fear through love. Unholiness breeds fear. But love conquers fear. in prayer we open our souls toward the love of Christ just as the flowers open themselves toward the sun. And, strange as it may seem, in the processes of daily living, we experience the victory over fear. "There is no fear in love, but perfect love casts out fear" (I John 4:18). This is true partly because in the love for God and neighbor we experience the confidence that comes from basic honesty. But it is also true because love coupled with faith is the best possible equipment for going into the future with God. Jesus said, " 'Fear not, little flock, for it is your Father's good pleasure to give you the kingdom' " (Luke 12:32). In that realm we gain the mastery over fear by the grace of God.

So, not by accident or stumbling through, but through prayer and faith, we gain peace and inner stability. Millions of people have experienced this peace and have borne witness to it; many have affirmed the power of prayer, even as they faced martyrdom and torture and persecution.

PRAYER AND LONELINESS

Loneliness is universal. Everybody knows what it is.

We may be seated in a room full of people and still feel lonely. We may be walking in a shopping center crowded with people and be overwhelmed with loneliness. We may have a husband or wife, children and grandchildren, friends and neighbors—each of whom we love—and still feel lonely. To be sure, this is not the same as the loneliness which comes when we have no one who is really close to us. But whether we have close family and friends or not, there is a mysterious sense of loneliness that haunts the human spirit. Each of us is a solitary soul. In a true sense, each of us is an island.

> Yes! in the sea of life enisl'd,
> With echoing straits between us thrown,
> Dotting the shoreless watery wild,
> We mortal millions live alone.
> (Matthew Arnold, "To Marguerite")

What is this loneliness of which the poets have spoken and of which I speak here? What is this solitariness that even the dearest lovers feel? And what is it that even our closest friends experience? It could be called the longing for God. Alfred North Whitehead meant far more than we are apt to suppose when he said, "Religion is what the individual does with his own solitariness." That idea is not the whole of religion; but it is certainly a part of it. Our solitariness does not drive us to God because we are left out of a social group. Nor is it that we are left out of a circle of intimate friends. Rather, it is the unalterable fact that each of us is walled into a private world. You are not I; I am not you.

We are born one by one and die one by one. Each has his or her own experiences. The feelings of each are private. And decisions, however influenced by circumstances or other people, are made by our individual wills. When we tie this fact of our solitariness to the fact of our finitude, we begin to get the message. Here let us change the figure from an island to a piece of cork bobbing up and down on an alien sea. No matter how many other corks there are, the ineradicable sense of our isolation is there. And this image suggests both our isolation and our flimsiness.

We may pause here to note that this isolation has nothing to do with whether we are male or female, black or white, yellow or red, ignorant or learned, rich or poor. It probes beneath the skin and goes beyond all cultural barriers. In fact, all those distinctions become relatively trivial and even comical when we consider this universal fact of solitariness. No man or woman on earth can ever escape the unalterable reality of this fundamental isolation.

Few things are more painful and destructive of human beings than the man-made injustices which breed on exclusiveness. In another dimension from this, think of the awful feeling of being thrown into an alien cosmic realm, alone, isolated, solitary. Here all alike may experience the sense of being lost in an apparently indifferent cosmos. I know of few thoughts more tragic than that of being an unknown entity in an unknowing universe.

What has all this to do with prayer? Everything. For loneliness, in its deeper dimensions, is the longing for God. It may even be one of the primary means by which the Holy Spirit summons us to open our souls to the living Word of God. People often ask, "Where is God? Why doesn't He make Himself known to me?" The answer is that God does make Himself known to each one of us. But we are blind and do not see, deaf and do not hear, stubborn and will not understand.

God is with us in our loneliness and solitariness drawing us toward the life-giving faith-relationship with Himself. It is as though God were saying to each of us, "Are you lonely, isolated? Then turn to your Maker in whom alone there can be enduring meaning." If you feel like a piece of cork tossed about on a stormy sea, then the Spirit of the living God is speaking to you, saying, "Come, son or daughter, behold my love for you in Jesus Christ, and put your trust in the One who is the Master of the storm-tossed sea."

In this mood, as we pray, the presence of the Holy Spirit is felt again and we know that we are not alone. For God is with us. In short, the mysterious sense of loneliness is God's call to commune with Him, to share with Him, to move with Him.

As we pray in our loneliness it is particularly important to have in mind certain great passages of the Bible. Not just any passages will do. For we require—in this deep mysterious experience of isolation—those passages in which the inspired writers felt what we feel. They too were profoundly lonely. Some of the most familiar parts of the Bible serve us well here.

Out of the depths I cry to thee, O Lord!

O Lord, thou hast searched me and known me!

Who shall separate us from the love of Christ?

The words of Jesus come home to us in these times of our loneliness: "Come to me, all who labor and are heavy laden, and I will give you rest" (Matt. 11:28).

"Peace I leave with you; my peace I give to you; not as the world gives do I give to you. Let not your hearts be troubled, neither let them be afraid" (John 14:27). ". . . and lo, I am with you always . . ." (Matt. 28:20).

Here too we find the meaning of many of the hymns which have stood the test of time. For their writers were keenly sensitive to this pervasive human condition of solitariness with its consequent sense of loneliness.

> A mighty fortress is our God,
> A bulwark never failing;
> Our helper he amid the flood
> Of mortal ills prevailing . . .
>
> Change and decay in all around I see;
> O thou who changest not, abide with me.*

Somewhere in here too we discover why private prayer is enriched abundantly by public worship. For the Holy Spirit works through the support systems of the community of prayer and faith to inform and quicken the Christian imagination. Then, in private prayer, the soul, as if it were nurtured and fed by the rich input of hymns, liturgy, sacraments, prayers, Scripture, preaching, and sharing, is prepared for God. In all of these, God's grace acts mysteriously to give us a more vital prayer-life. And our solitary souls thus open themselves to the enduring, joy-creating fellowship with God through Jesus Christ.

Herein also lies the reason why we cannot help but love God, if we know who He is and how much He

---

*"O Love that wilt not let me go,
I rest my weary soul in thee . . ."

cares for each of us. Most of the time we human beings never see God. We see the world around us. We see other people; at least we see their bodies. But we do not think about who God really is. We have eyes but do not see, ears but do not hear. Then, in certain holy moments, the veil is removed and we get a vision of God. We behold Him as perfect love. We know Him as the One who created us out of that love. We see Him in His perfection and unutterable glory. We know Him as the Fountain of all possibilities of grace in Jesus Christ. And when this happens, we cannot help but love God.

When we see a rose, we delight in it. When we see the mountains in their fall glory—spread out before us like a magnificent garden of colors—we feel their splendor. When we see the starry heavens, we stand in awe. And when we lift up our heads and are given the eyes of faith to behold the glory of God, we cannot help but love and adore Him. More than that, we cannot help but serve God.

Sometimes such a vision may come to us in the solitariness of our private devotions; sometimes, in the fellowship with other believers; sometimes, during public worship when we hear the Word, sing the hymns, and feel the power of each other's prayers. But for all who truly seek, God graciously grants the assurance of His Presence, and we know that we are not alone.

PRAYER AND TEMPTATION

Temptation is fascination with the destructive. A desire for anything good is not usually considered temptation. We do not think of the desire for truth, or goodness, or beauty as temptation. Nor do we think that when a person wants a good job, he or she is being tempted. Temptation is desire, but, as we are considering it here, it is desire for the wrong thing. In Milton's *Paradise Lost*, when Eve took the fruit, she was convinced that she was choosing good.

On the face of it, it would seem that people would not want anything which is harmful or destructive. But this is not the case. We human beings are so made that we tend to see only the delights of a particular act and lose sight of the damaging consequences. We can easily talk ourselves into supposing that there will be no such consequences. And sometimes, even when we know we will be bringing harm to ourselves and to those we love, we go ahead in our folly. Often we live in a fool's paradise and become *victims of the tyranny of the immediate present*. This is why I speak of temptation as the fascination with the destructive—which is not at the moment seen as destructive.

Human nature is a curious thing. It has an inexhaustible capacity to be fascinated or bewitched by what strikes against it. Freud's talk about a "death instinct"—which seems to be a kind of death-wish—is more real than we might like to believe. And who can number the people who work incessantly for what leads to their own unhappiness! Therefore, it is no accident that the biblical writers recognized the importance of coming to grips with temptation. The work of Moses and the prophets was in no small degree concerned with the never-ending problem of Israel's temptation to turn away from the Lord God by lapsing into idolatry and immorality. Jesus warned against yielding to temptation. And he told about those who quickly respond to the Word of God but who, having no root, "in time of temptation fall away" (Luke 8:13).

The Master included temptation in the great prayer he left with His disciples. No one seems to know quite how to interpret the words: "And lead us not into temptation." For we cannot understand how the Father would actually lead His children into temptation. And if He does lead us into temptation, we have to ask, Why pray not to be so led? Here we do well to remember the words of the Epistle of James: "Let no one say when he is tempted, 'I am tempted by God'; for God cannot be tempted with evil and He Himself tempts no one; but each person is tempted when he is lured and enticed by his own desire" (James 1:13-14).

Whatever else Jesus meant, we note that He moved from the words about temptation to those about deliverance: "But deliver us from evil." In our Lord's Prayer, then, we find the longing for victory over temptation expressed in the powerful petition for deliverance from evil.

In the biblical context there are two reasons why we should pray to overcome temptation. The first is to avoid the harmful consequences of evil deeds. The second is to grow spiritually through the experience of gaining the victory over temptation. Let us consider these briefly.

Our heavenly Father calls us to prayer before the times of temptation so that we may avoid the destructive consequences of wrongdoing. Jesus said to His drowsy disciples, "Why do you sleep? Rise and pray that you may not enter into temptation" (Luke 22:46). Here is the suggestion that through prayer we are so prepared in advance that no strong temptation will have sway over us. This is undoubtedly one of the soundest principles of the spiritual life. A person who waits to pray until the temptations come is almost sure to fail. But whoever follows Jesus by preparing in advance through prayer and faith has already gained the victory with God's help.

The words of Paul bear on this too. He said: "Therefore let any one who thinks that he stands take heed lest he fall. No temptation has overtaken you that is not common to man. God is faithful, and he will not let you be tempted beyond your strength, but with the temptation will also provide the way of escape, that you may be able to endure it" (I Cor. 10:12-13). Paul's words have as much relevance today as they did for the Christians at Corinth. These verses indicate that we become strong through encounters with temptation. We as Christians are to live the new life in the world where our temptations take us. This does not mean that we are to engage in a weak and sentimental flirting with temptation. Rather, it means that in life itself temptation is inevitable; and we grow spiritually through the encounters with it. It is no sin to be tempted. Jesus was tempted (Matt. 4:1-11). He was ". . . in every respect . . . tempted as we are, yet without sin" (Heb. 4:15). The sin comes from *not being prepared in advance to rise above temptation.*

In this context temptation is not merely the alluring destructive; it is also the opportunity for victory. Temptation is God's way of testing us and seeing what we are made of. So temptation confronts us with a danger to be avoided and, at the same time, a challenge to be faced. In the Epistle of James we read in this connection: "Count it all joy, my brethren, when you meet various trials, for you know that the testing of your faith produces steadfastness. And let steadfastness have its full effect, that you may be perfect and complete, lacking in nothing" (James 1:2-4). But here again it is assumed that those who meet these trials and temptations successfully will do so with God's help. Hence, prayer.

The need for prayer is all the more evident when we note that during some of our moods we are almost sure to falter and stumble before temptation. For example, when we have been terribly disappointed, and our world has collapsed around us, we are apt to sink like stones in the face of temptations of one sort or another. Sustained anxiety also tends to incapacitate us for victory. Kierkegaard went so far as to say that anxiety is the primal source of sin. Grief and tragedy often make us vulnerable. And sometimes poor health causes us to lose morale before the challenges of life.

Morale is the will to adventure. It means entering upon each day with hope and promise. But there are many times and circumstances when we are so overwhelmed by events, so shattered by grief, and so confused by anxiety that we are temptation-prone. In such times and moods we need especially to pray for God's help in order to be more than conquerors through faith in Christ. The power of God "is made perfect in weakness" (II Cor. 12:9). And we come to know through prayer what Paul had in mind when he said, "When I am weak, then I am strong" (II Cor. 12:10). That is, when we realize we need God's help, we are on our way toward moral and spiritual strength.

In and through it all, we look to Jesus Christ because He is the source and "perfecter of our faith"

(Heb. 12:2). We look to Him because He is the conqueror of the severest temptations. And we can draw near to the throne of grace with confidence "that we may receive mercy and find grace to help in time of need" (Heb. 4:16).

In this connection, the word "grace" is one of the most beautiful words in the New Testament. Paul, more than any other, put it into our Christian vocabulary. What does it mean? "Grace" means God's immediate presence and power at work in us through Jesus Christ. God is gracious. But His grace is not what He does for Himself or to Himself. God's grace is His love and power flowing into and through our souls. God graciously pardons our sins. God's act of pardoning us through the merits of Jesus Christ is not experienced by us because it is *God's* act—experienced by Him alone. Rather His presence as the pardoning God is *in us*—experienced by us, witnessed by us. In times of temptation, when we feel our frailty and hold fast to Christ, we experience the inflowing grace of God and are given the power to look temptation in the face and drive it away.

God's grace that is in us is incomparably greater than the evil forces in the world around us. As the inspired writer put it: "Greater is he that is in you, than he that is in the world" (I John 4:4 KJV).

PRAYER AND SUFFERING

There are times when prayer is the only thing that can keep us going. Matthew Arnold observed that the ancient Greeks, in their religion, assumed that people were never sick or sorry. But the sense of tragedy moves through the Judeo-Christian heritage like a mighty theme. The episodes of biblical history are perpetual reminders that sorrow, suffering, pain, spiritual disaster, and death are substantive factors in the history of Israel as well as in the lives of the apostles and other Christians. Rachel weeping for her children and the prophets suffering for their convictions tell the story.

Jesus came on the scene not as the "happy warrior," but as the Suffering Servant. "He was despised and rejected by men; a man of sorrows, and acquainted with grief" (Isa. 53:3).

God does not promise us that, when we put our trust in Him, everything will work out all right on earth. Neither the prophets nor Jesus had an easy time of it. And the apostles encountered sorrow, suffering, and martyrdom.

Why do people suffer? Or, why do the innocent suffer? There is no adequate answer to those questions. Sometimes we suffer because of our sins and mistakes, sometimes, because of the sin and folly of others. But often we suffer without any justifiable reason. All we can say is that we know God is good, we know He loves us and suffers with us, and gives us the strength we need in the midst of our suffering and grief. When we look at life itself, we realize how often tragedy overtakes us. We can easily understand what an anonymous actor felt when he said, "The theater of all my acts has fallen." If we are spared for a time, we still know that suffering is sure to come. For death is inevitable. And that means the loss of those with whom our lives have been woven together in love and friendship for many years. Memories of those precious ones may linger, but they are as mere shadows compared to the touch of a hand, the sound of a voice, the warmth of a presence.

How can the shattered relationships be mended when death has had its say? Can we pick up the fragments of our broken dreams and start over? Can the love and friendship of a lifetime be begun again when the evening is drawing near? No. What then? Has the God who made us forsaken us? Has the Christ who redeemed us cast us off? Has the Holy Spirit who comforted us abandoned us? God forbid. What then?

Our heavenly Father, in His infinite love and wisdom, has made provision for us in the hours of our suffering and grief. He summons us to enter into an ever-renewing faith in Him. He calls us to prayer. And when, amid our suffering and grief, we open our souls to Him in prayer, we receive at least four blessings of supreme importance.

The first is that, despite our sorrow and grief, we become more profoundly aware of the presence of God. Whereas earlier in life, when all seemed to be going well, we could question God's love, doubt His purpose for us, and neglect His resources, we no longer do so. In the depths of our weakness and inadequacy, God has given us the vision of His glory and the warmth of His presence. We *know*, as millions before us have known, that the Father will never leave us or forsake us. For He made us and we are His people, the sheep of His pasture (Ps. 100:3). Therefore, through suffering and grief, God works to perfect His own and to make Himself ever present.

Closely related to this is a second blessing from our prayer-life that God brings through suffering and grief, namely, a more profound awareness of the height and depth and riches of God's glory and grace. It is one thing to know that God goes with us through life and tragedy and death. It is another thing to become increasingly aware of the vast ranges of God's mysterious love in redeeming, nurturing, and empowering us for mission. Paul, who knew suffering, caught something of the spirit of this when he cried:

O the depth of the riches and wisdom and knowledge of God! How unsearchable are his judgments and how inscrutable his ways!

"For who has known the mind of the Lord,
or who has been his counselor?
Or who has given a gift to him
that he might be repaid?"

For from him and through him and to him are all things. To him be glory for ever. Amen. (Romans 11:33-36)

Out of the depths of suffering and grief comes the vision of the greatness and glory of God. And in Him we are enabled to sing again.

In times of suffering a third special blessing comes to us, namely, through the prayers and presence of others we receive a new appreciation of the care and support which comes from the fellowship of believers. In the church we find that others are caring for us and suffering with us. And the Holy Spirit mysteriously uses their comforting hands and prayers to give us the grace to see life through. Then, as we pray during the lonely hours of the night, we thank God for the ties that bind our hearts in Christian love and for the sympathizing tear.

A fourth blessing of prayer in the times of suffering is the new vision of service. When we have lost all—or what seems like all—the Father graciously opens up avenues of service on which we can move into the future. He makes us aware that as long as we are on earth, as long as we are called upon to live and breathe, we are summoned by God to do what we can to help others.

All who have known grief are placed in a special position to help others who grieve. All who have suffered greatly may feel more deeply than others the hurt of human beings and enter upon the life of service with a greater capacity for sympathy and for thoughtful deeds. When we suffer real tragedy, we receive new priorities, new values, new ways of understanding the difference between what is important and what is trivial. This too, by God's grace, gives us the power to serve more productively and creatively in God's holy mission.

In short, we behold anew the glory of God in Jesus Christ who came not to be ministered to but to serve. Then, by the grace of God, we strive to walk as Jesus walked. And when our life on earth is done, we know that we shall have an opportunity for an everlasting adventure with God and with all who love Him in the life after death. We can live with the hope of being reunited with those we love. For we know that God is not encouraging us to form beautiful friendships on earth only to see them destroyed by death.

PRAYER AND SCIENCE

There are many sciences—astronomy, geology, physics, chemistry, biology, biochemistry, microbiology, psychology, social sciences, *et cetera*. They are known as sciences because they share in the determination to practice methods of verification which are considered essential for arriving at truth. The sciences, though differing widely in fields of specialization, are similar in the steps required for verifying their theories. They begin with a problem to be investigated. They proceed by collecting data, suggesting hypotheses, performing relevant experiments, testing and retesting the hypotheses, and arriving at conclusions drawn from the total process.

It would not be going too far to say that the discovery of the scientific method is one of the finest achievements of human beings. It has freed us from numberless superstitions regarding diseases, natural disasters, future events, and environmental realities. It has made possible thousands upon thousands of conveniences and technologically based inventions, tools, and machines that save the time and energy of people around the world. Science and technology together have allowed us to envision realistically a world free from poverty, famine, and major diseases. The future of our world depends on the uses made of the many discoveries laid before the nations. Are the advances in chemistry to be used for chemical warfare? Are the nuclear arsenals to be developed and used for destroying people and their cities?

What has all this to do with prayer? A great deal. According to many thinkers today—including some scientists and philosophers—prayer is considered superstitious. To be sure, there have been outstanding scientists in the past who believed in God and the life of prayer. So is it with many first-rate scientists and philosophers today. But there are many who believe that there is no scientific or rational basis for the practice of prayer. And for that reason they rule it out. In addition to many scholars who are either agnostics or philosophical naturalists, there are multitudes of others who, though not technically trained in the sciences, live in an atmosphere of doubt which leaves no place for prayer. They may say "yes" to meditation, but "no" to prayer. There are several reasons why many people feel this way.

Those who breathe the atmosphere of doubt which pervades our culture seem to me to be what Wesley called "practical atheists." Even though they may believe in some kind of God, they act as if God did not exist. Another way of putting it is this: Many people are secularists. As I am using that term here, a secularist is one who believes that if God is, He doesn't matter.

Consider now the many scientists and philosophers who have no place for prayer in their outlook and practice. One reason for thinking as they do is that they are so impressed with the advances made by the sciences that they minimize or even exclude other avenues of arriving at truth. Therefore, they assume that any beliefs not derived from scientific method and direct observation are to be laid aside.

Moreover, many scientists are apt to forget the limitations that scientific method imposes upon itself. Among these is the confinement to limited areas of investigation. Each of the sciences proceeds by restricting radically its focus. Consequently, each deals only with *aspects* or *fragments* of reality. Each science shuts out the total realms of reality which lie around its special focus. In this way, the ultimate questions are thrust aside as though they were irrelevant.

Alfred North Whitehead made much of this. Science is made possible because of the ordered processes with which it deals. This is assumed in all types of experimentation and laboratory work. But how do we explain an ordered universe when there are infinite possibilities for chaos? There is no reason why scientists and theologians might not join hands in believing in the Ultimate Mind who created and orders the universe and its varied and intricate processes. And whenever this happens, at least there is an open door to prayer for those who so believe.

Closely related to these considerations is another factor of some importance. There are areas of reality and truth other than those with which the sciences deal. To be sure, scientists are fully aware of the extensive areas of potential knowledge not yet attained by the sciences. There are vast realms of unknowns. For example, what is the so-called "dark matter" of which some astronomers speak? We are told that those parts of the universe which we can see are 90 percent hydrogen. But "dark matter" makes up 90 percent of the universe. And we do not know what "dark matter" consists of. Is it some element not known to us now? Or, is there such a realm of reality at all? We do not know. There are numberless gaps or chasms yet to be explored or which may never be explored. This fact has led some cynical scholars to say that religious people hold on to a "god of the gaps." As scientific knowledge advances—so they have said—we keep receding into the realms of the unknown and hold that *there* is where God is still at work. So we Christians are charged with using God to fill in the vast chasms of our ignorance.

In response to this charge, two comments are in order. First, sound thought leads us to see clearly that these chasms of ignorance are in our lack of knowledge, not in the universe itself. Ultimately viewed, the God who created and sustains the universe acts in it and through it, in all of its known and unknown processes, to produce the whole ordered realm of reality. A "god of the gaps" is no god at all. Besides this, the assumption that as we do away with the gaps of ignorance there will be less and less point in talking about God reveals monumental superficiality of understanding. For our best thinking leads us to see that any ordered universe requires the ultimate ordering Mind or Intelligence to explain its existence and processes.

The second comment is that there are dimensions of reality that may not be discoverable by the methods of the sciences. Why should we assume that scientific methods alone lead human beings to orient themselves rightly to reality? There may be realms of reality that may never be discovered by the sciences. Music, poetry, novels, drama, linguistics, history, and philosophical and theological reflections deal in reality also. And the saints have reported on what they have confirmed in the ongoing of their lives as the reality, presence, and power of God in prayer.

We are never justified in ruling out the realm of God's grace because we do not see how it can be made accessible to the sciences. When it comes to prayer, we move into a different realm from what can be scientifically verified. The realities of prayer cannot be stated in mathematical formulas. They cannot be put into test tubes or laid out on the tables of anatomy. Those who have experimented most persistently and resourcefully in the life of prayer speak most authoritatively on the subject. Everything here depends on the reality and love of God. If God is, and if He cares, then the doors to prayer are wide open. And all are invited to "taste and see that the Lord is good."

It is evident to me that there is no conflict between the faith that leads to the life of prayer and the whole realm of scientific truth.

UNANSWERED PRAYER

The great characters of the Bible were all familiar with the disconcerting experience of unanswered prayer. Moses prayed for God to let him go over the Jordan River into the Promised Land, but God did not grant his petition (Deut. 3:23-27). This is exceedingly baffling to us when we consider all that Moses had done to deliver the people from slavery and to lead them creatively through the wilderness for forty years. If it happened to Moses, it can happen to us.

Job knew about unanswered prayer:

> I cry to thee and thou dost not
> answer me;
> I stand, and thou dost not heed
> me. (30:20)

The psalmist said that God hides himself in times of trouble (10:1). Again, we read:

> O my God, I cry by day, but thou
> dost not answer;
> and by night, but find no rest. (22:2)

God spoke to Isaiah saying,

> When you spread forth your hands,
>   I will hide my eyes from you;
> even though you make many
>   prayers,
>   I will not listen;
>   your hands are full of blood. (1:15)

Jeremiah added his word when he reported what the Lord told him: "Though Moses and Samuel stood before me, yet my heart would not turn toward this people. Send them out of my sight, and let them go!" (15:1).

In the New Testament also we read of this same experiment of unanswered prayer. Jesus Himself prayed at Gethsemane saying, "My Father, if it be possible, let this cup pass from me . . ." (Matt. 26:39). Paul prayed three times for God to remove what he called a "thorn in the flesh." But that petition was denied him (II Cor. 12:7-8). If this happened to Jesus and Paul, it can happen to us.

Christians on all levels of spirituality—including the saints—have shared in this experience of unanswered prayer. What are we to say about it? Are there any illuminating insights? The plain fact is that we cannot add much to what has been said already on this subject. Nevertheless, we may refresh our minds by looking at some of the ideas with which we are already familiar.

For one thing, everyone knows that there is such a thing as insincere prayer. Those who pray falsely do not really love God and neighbor. They do not truly want God's will to be done in them. Instead, because of some personal concern or danger from which they want to be delivered, they send out desperate prayers to God. In their desperation they may even make promises to God which they are not apt to keep. Only God can judge whether or not a prayer is sincere. Sometimes our prayers are mere words which we repeat ceremoniously. Jesus said, "And in praying do not heap up empty phrases as the Gentiles do; for they think that they will be heard for their many words" (Matt. 6:7). In the light of Christ, we know that this much is sure: No prayer is fully authentic that is not based on His command to pray for God's kingdom to come and for His will to be done on earth as it is in heaven.

Perhaps our prayers are not answered because we are unwilling to do our part. We pray God to forgive us for our sins. But we have not really decided to change our evil ways. Or, we have ignored the demands of Jesus, who said that if we are unwilling to forgive others who have wronged us, then God will not pardon our sins. We have to ask ourselves again and again whether we are actually praying in the name or spirit of the Master.

Or maybe when we pray we ask God to do for us what God expects us to do for ourselves. There are many things which God never intended us to receive through prayer. For they must be the products of our own efforts. We should pray for daily bread, but that is no substitute for the skill of the farmers who cultivate the soil, plant the seeds, and bring in the harvest. And that prayer is not commanded to make us neglect the God-ordained trips to the grocery stores.

I shall never forget the time when, as a ministerial student, I was praying earnestly for higher levels of Christian experience. As I did, the sure impression was given me by the Holy Spirit that I was expecting God to create Christian growth without my own creative efforts. God has given us minds to be used, hearts to be made alive, and wills to be set in motion. That was for me a real moment of illumination. Wesley was right when he said that a growing Christian is a Christian who keeps learning and reading. God never intended for prayer to be a substitute for the hard tasks of thinking and working. At the same time, these are no substitutes for the divine grace which comes to us through prayer.

And it may be that we do not receive what we ask for because we are not ready for it. God knows the stages of our spiritual development and He may hold in reserve His responses until we have grown to adulthood. A little girl might ask for food which her mother knows she is not ready to digest. God, in His infinite love and goodness, may give an answer to prayer by saying, "Not yet," "not now."

How often it is that we pray for things and experiences which we would not know how to handle if we got them! A little boy might pray for a machine gun, but he ought not to have it. So it can be with the petitions of adults. Are we really ready for what we are praying for? That question is often overlooked. Frequently we do not know what to pray for because we do not know what we most need. In some moods we want one thing, in other moods we want the opposite. What would happen if God were to answer our every whim which comes to utterance in prayer! Our limited understanding—nay, our ignorance—is surely a factor in unanswered prayer. Oscar Wilde had a point when he said, "When the gods wish to punish us, they answer our prayers" (*An Ideal Husband*). How often we are ruined by our own wishes!

Another thing to bear in mind is that God takes the laws of nature seriously. He established them and shows no signs of doing away with them. Fortunately for us, we can rely on the functioning of these steadfast ordinances. Of course, God's actions are not confined to the laws of nature, for God's grace moves dynamically beyond the realm of physical processes. But God does not defy His own ordered systems. Therefore, some prayers are not answered simply because, if they were, the ordered universe would be disrupted. God wants us to live in full respect for the laws of nature which are essential to our health and well-being.

The most important thing to remember about unanswered prayer is that it concerns only a small part of true prayer. Petition is only one part of prayer. In defining prayer we noted that it is essentially communion and encounter with God. If this is so, then almost all sincere prayers are answered. For those who truly seek God in the right way find Him. They walk with God, commune with God, and glory in God's presence. To be sure, there are times when God seems to hide His face from them. There is "the dark night of the soul" of which the saints have spoken. But, as people persist in prayer, the new day dawns and God is again known and felt to be present in peace, joy, confrontation, and inner witness.

We may say, then, that when we do our part there are some kinds of prayers which are always answered. One of these is the prayer for a life surrendered to and placed at the disposal of our heavenly Father. Another prayer which is invariably answered whenever we fulfill the conditions is the prayer for a life-long faith-relationship with God through Christ. Still another prayer which is always answered, when we do our part, is the prayer for forgiveness. "If we confess our sins, he is faithful and just, and will forgive our sins and cleanse us from all unrighteousness" (I John 1:9). And the prayer for empowerment by the Holy Spirit so we can more effectively do the work of the kingdom is always answered.

I believe the main reason for unanswered prayer is that we do not really pray for the things we most need. We have not, because we ask not. The most important answer to prayer is the closer walk with God and the desire to know and do God's will.

CHAPTER FOUR

Prayer and Creative Living

PRAYER AND THE MEANING OF LIFE

In moments of prayer we have direct experiences of the meaning and glory of life. For there we know that God is with us, that He cares, and that what we think and do really matters. In prayer, then, the whole sweep of revealed religion becomes an experienced reality.

One of the deepest and most insistent questions we ask is this: Does life have any enduring meaning? Sometimes we ask it in relation to death. In that case it takes one of the following forms: What is the meaning of life in the face of a sure death? If at death we end up at zero, how can we make sense out of our lives? What difference does anything make in the end?

Across many centuries some of the greatest thinkers have devoted long and painful hours to these questions. Some have said that life is absurd, meaningless, without any enduring significance. Others have insisted that each human life has meaning both in itself and, more basically, in relation to God's revealed purpose for us.

It was one of the tragedies of the twentieth century that, as it moved from decade to decade, it failed to produce many strong philosophical minds who support the idea that human life has enduring meaning and glory. Consequently, we may say with regret that many of the philosophers of our time have offered very little help on this important issue. It strikes me as completely unsatisfying to believe with the process-theologians that our only enduring meaning is in our contribution to God's enrichment. In that perspective, we have no enduring selfhood, no soul which can pass beyond death into eternal life. The sacred line of self-identity is obliterated at death. Where then is the enduring meaning of our souls?

On this theme the philosophers known as Personalists have more to offer than any others. And their total world-view, with the personal God as the only ultimate reality and with each human being as a person, is on the side of the biblical revelation. For the Bible is a book about the personal God who *knows* us, *loves* us, *redeems* us, and *communes* with us. And we are creatures of unutterable worth. For we were created by God to exist as living individual souls with the power to think, feel, and act.

At a meeting of the American Philosophical Association several years ago, one session was devoted to "the meaning of life." It attracted wide interest. Many of the philosophers from the eastern colleges and universities in the United States were there. And nearly all of them attended this plenary session. The main lecture was delivered by a philosopher from Princeton University. He developed the ancient theme that our life has no enduring meaning. By prearrangement two philosophers responded as critics. One of these, a philosopher from Harvard University, urged that, on the contrary, life has meaning. We *experience* this, he said. We know that it does matter as to whether we do a just or unjust act. But even he concluded by suggesting that in the end life has little meaning. "For," he said, "if God is, I would expect him to take an unexcited view of man."

As scores of the philosophers laughed, I thought of the whole sweep of revealed religion. I thought of the prophets who reminded the people of Israel of God's concern for them in His covenantal relationship. I thought of Jesus Christ and his passion for "one of the least." I thought of the vast Christian movement with its prayers, hymns, sacraments, symbols, preaching, devotional services, and its saints. Then I said to myself, "That's it! The essence of Christianity—on one side of it—is precisely *that God takes an excited view of each human being.*" So, while we may sit at the feet of philosophers and learn some things, we kneel at the foot of the Cross and celebrate. Celebrate what? The mysterious, glorious fact that the infinite God of this universe, our Father, created each one of us for an enduring meaning. What could not be discovered by man's reason has been revealed in God's Word. And this revelation becomes an experienced reality when God meets us in prayer.

The biblical revelation, from one standpoint, is a vast succession of events and utterances on the dignity, meaning, and glory of human life under God. It never lapses into the arrogant and degrading notion that man can be or do anything apart from God. But it constantly urges that our life is important to God, that He cares about the way we live, and that He wants us to work with Him and others in the realization of values. That is, the Bible is a vast and inspired summons to join with God in doing a great work in the Kingdom. Jesus taught this clearly, simply, and profoundly.

The Christian communities of prayer and faith, for all their imperfections, are divinely inspired media for telling the good news of this biblical affirmation of the meaning and dignity of each human being. The very thought—made explicit in preaching, teaching, singing, praying, and serving others—that God cared enough to give Himself in Jesus Christ in our behalf tells the story. God takes an excited view of each human being: "While we were yet sinners Christ died for us" (Rom. 5:8).

An understanding of the meaning and preciousness of our souls comes home to each of us in prayer. Here we know that God is with us in all that we are and do. No matter what our failures and weaknesses may be, we are assured in prayer by the inner witness that God's love is real and our love for Him and for our fellow human beings is important.

In prayer and worship we *have the only concrete experience of the enduring meaning of our lives on earth.* We pass from the theoretical to the practical, from thought to life. Surely one of the most important motives for praying and worshiping is to experience for ourselves the peace and joy of knowing that what we are and do matters. For God is with us, delights in us, and empowers us *for* service and *in* service. The significance of a vital prayer-life for experiencing the sense of life's enduring meaning cannot be exaggerated. Intellectual reflection helps us to ground our faith rationally. But life is deeper than logic. And what the Bible reveals about God's work in us is confirmed in our ongoing experiences in prayer and worship.

Four affirmations are foundational in our Christian understanding of prayer and the meaning of life. The first is that God exists and cares for each human being. Without this certainty there is no ultimate basis for hope or meaning in our passing careers on earth. Prayer changes this basic tenet from a merely intellectual affirmation into an experienced reality.

The second foundational affirmation is this: The God who created and sustains the universe has revealed His love for each person through Jesus Christ, the Son of God, who lived, died, and was raised from the dead that all might have everlasting life. This revelation could not have been made with such power, beauty, and sublimity by words alone. Therefore, God took the initiative in Jesus Christ, the Living Word, to make known His unalterable love for us. This too becomes personally real in our hearts through prayer.

The third foundational affirmation essential to the Christian understanding of the meaning of life is that each human being is a soul created in the image of God and made for an everlasting destiny. There are many modern perspectives on our human nature according to which the soul is conspicuous by its absence. There may be successions of states of consciousness. But even these are often analyzed into brain-processes. It strikes me as strange that men and women of intellectual acumen would be willing to advance complicated theories that reduce human beings to chemical processes, or to brain processes, or to anything that is merely physical. The fatal flaw here is to assume that because we can identify causal connections between the brain, nervous system, and chemicals, on the one hand, and our thoughts, emotions, and acts, on the other, the two are the same. But it should be intuitively evident that what *causes* or *affects* the mind is one thing and the mind itself is another. Long before we knew about these causal connections in detail, Homer wrote his *Iliad*, Paul wrote his Epistle to the Romans, and Columbus set out on his grand voyage of discovery.

A human being is not merely an animal among animals—the fortuitous product of blind chance. A human being is a living soul made for an everlasting destiny with God. One would think that the most capable minds in the world would be doing everything they could, with solid reasons, to show the preciousness and dignity of each human being. But this would not be possible by any theory which reduces the soul to something physical. The reality of all this becomes a part of our very existence through prayer.

The fourth foundational affirmation essential to the Christian understanding of the meaning of life is that when our present bodies die our souls live on. The human soul is not its body or any part of its body. These two, body and soul (or mind), are intimately and causally interrelated. The soul affects the body and the body the soul. But they are distinct realities. Therefore, when the body has served its purpose and dies, this does not mean the death of the soul. The God who in this life made possible the marvelous interconnections between our souls and bodies can certainly ensure the soul's pilgrimage in the life to come. Everything here depends on God's holy purpose for us. God has revealed this in the resurrection of Jesus. And we experience in prayer the unbreakable bonds of God's love. In prayer we are assured of the everlasting adventures with God in His heavenly kingdom.

PRAYER AND DESIRE

In this chapter I propose to consider in some detail prayer and our supreme desire as Christians: the love of God and neighbor. Then, since God wants us to express our Christian love in creative working relationships with this present life, we shall consider the following topics: prayer and family life, prayer and work, prayer and leisure, and prayer and public worship. Let us turn to these in that order.

Desire is the engine of life. Without it we can do nothing. For desire sets us in motion. When Buddha went into the world away from his princely setting, he encountered sickness, old age, and death. Then he felt driven to go out on a pilgrimage in search of the answer to suffering. Finally he said that desire is the source of all human suffering. Therefore we should do what we can to rid ourselves of desire.

Jesus taught that desire is at the heart of our very existence. He assumed that God made us desiring beings. In one of His parables of the Kingdom, Jesus told of a man who found a treasure hidden in a field and sold everything he had so he could buy that field. The kingdom of God is realized when we desire totally what God most wants (see Matt. 13:44).

Jesus said that the two major problems with desire are wrong desire, on the one hand, and the conflict of desires, on the other. As to the first, he said, "For out of the heart come evil thoughts, murder, adultery, fornication, theft, false witness, slander" (Matt. 15:19).

The word "heart" in this context refers to the center and source of our being. And this concerns not only our thoughts and feelings, but our desires. Wrong desires inevitably produce evil thoughts and actions. The bad tree produces bad fruit, the sound tree, good fruit (Matt. 7:17-18). "The good man out of the good treasure of his heart produces good, and the evil man out of his evil treasure produces evil" (Luke 6:45).

All of this implies the Master's call to pray for purity of heart. Then and only then will the desires in our hearts glorify God and bless others. Through prayer God graciously purifies our souls and enables us to be dominated by the supreme desire, namely, the love of God and neighbor.

Jesus knew also that desires may conflict with each other and incapacitate us for service to God. There is always the problem of the soul divided against itself. Jesus put it this way: "No one can serve two masters; for either he will hate the one and love the other, or he will be devoted to the one and despise the other. You cannot serve God and mammon" (Matt. 6:24).

The reality of this kind of deep-seated dynamic conflict calls for prayer. In times of prayer we are aware of the war between good and evil within us. And the Holy Spirit makes us see our pride, selfishness, and love of the world. We know that these inner evil desires are dragging us away from God. So we pray for God to give us the love of Christ which drives away all evil desires.

Paul brought a new light on the relationship between prayer and our desires. He led us to pray for the spiritual resources which are available *through faith in Christ*. Paul did more than any of the earliest Christians to emphasize the organic connection between our prayer-life and the dynamic presence of the Risen Christ. What the strict practice of the religion of the Pharisees could not do for Paul, Christ did. After his encounter with the Risen Lord, Paul experienced the life-transforming *power* for which he longed. Therefore, he testified boldly that Christ was the supreme motivating power within him (Phil. 1:21; see I Cor. 2:2; Gal. 2:20). He received from Christ, through the Holy Spirit, the power to fulfill God's holy purpose for him, whether in tent-making, preaching, teaching, writing, or in establishing local churches. It was the supernatural grace of God in Christ that flooded his soul with that supreme desire, the love of God and neighbor.

No wonder Paul said, "For the kingdom of God does not consist in talk but in power" (I Cor. 4:20; see I Thess. 1:5). In keeping with this, he referred to the gospel as "the power of God for salvation" (Rom. 1:16). He wanted the faith of the Corinthians to rest not on human wisdom "but in the power of God" (I Cor. 2:5).

Among our most important personal relationships during our life on earth are those in the family. We are born into families. We marry into families. We have children in families. We desire for our family relationships those Christian qualities which make for peace, joy, and creative efforts together. It is not easy to manifest the Christian virtues in all situations at home. Therefore, we need to pray for God's grace in Christ. What specifically should we pray for? For the forgiving spirit; for the understanding heart; for the love of Christ toward each member of the family; for the grace to hold fast to those we love when we are tempted to give up on them; and, when the situation demands it, for tough love, straight talk, and forthright action. In and through all situations, our prayer should be for the earnest *desire* for God's best for each member of the family.

Work is an important part of life. The deep *desire* to accomplish something burns like a divine flame in nearly every human being. And this bears directly on finding our place in the work-force of the world. Discovering our vocation in life is not easy. A few people realize what they want to do in life in their childhood or youth and they get on with it. Others experience periods of trial and error. Still others face times of counseling, guidance, and extended education.

How can prayer have a part in our work for a living? In several ways.

For one thing, when we pray about our work we come to think of it as a vocation—a calling from God—and not merely a job. This implies a willingness to open our understanding to the guidance of the Holy Spirit. Divine guidance is always to be tested by the realities of life, but we are ever to be open to the movement of the Spirit. For God cares about the work we do for a living.

For another thing, as we pray, God helps us to identify our talents, gifts, and training, and to aim them toward work that is in demand. All kinds of worthy work are needed in the world. But our work needs to be suited to our abilities, interests, and education. It would have been tragic in the extreme for Moses, who was trained in Pharoah's palaces, to have continued to look after Jethro's sheep, goats, and cattle. So God called him to lead the people of Israel out of their bondage to the Egyptians.

Through prayer God gives us morale in our work. God helps us to delight in work. God helps us to see and appreciate the privilege of work and of receiving the money earned by it. Work can become a burden. It sometimes loses its glory when it is reduced to routines. But through prayer all that is changed. For we are working for the glory of God. And the money earned is a blessing from God which is to be used by ourselves and our families as faithful stewards.

Through prayer we see that God hates needless unemployment. Few things are more tragic than being unemployed when we want and need work. This does not mean that we are necessarily bound to do only that work with which we began. There may come a time for a change in our vocation. In that event we must consider prayerfully the basic questions: What further training do I need to qualify? Whom should I consult? What do the other members of the family think? Will it involve an acceptable or unacceptable move to another community?

Through prayer we develop the desire to do our best work. For our work is done for the glory of God and for the blessing of people. This burning God-given desire requires concentration. It demands the willingness to focus on whatever is needed to improve our workmanship. Thomas Edison asked one of his assistants whether or not he believed in luck. The assistant answered: "Yes and no." Edison then said, "For my part, I don't believe in luck at all." He added, "Most fellows try a few things and then quit. I never quit until I get what I'm after. That's the only difference between me, that's supposed to be lucky, and the fellows that think they are unlucky." He said that many people think that things are just going to work by themselves. We must always remember that nothing worthwhile comes by itself, just to please us. We have to make it work.

Some people destroy themselves by overwork. Neither their bodies nor their minds can take the beating they inflict. Our time and energy need to be measured. The most prayerful action anyone can take who is physically and mentally exhausted is to have a planned withdrawal from work. That planned withdrawal may be brief or extended, depending on the need. Therefore, another important dimension of the Christian life is leisure time. I include in this the times of humor, of pleasing games, of physical exercise, of entertainment through music, drama, and art, of fellowship with friends, and of the privilege of simply gazing on beautiful things and scenes. We should pray especially for a healthy sense of humor. The ability to laugh at ourselves is very close to the heart of God.

Sometimes our leisure time may be set apart almost spontaneously. Most of the time we will want to pray about it and discuss it with all who are involved. In this way, planned leisure time can give us the changes most needed so we can return to our work refreshed. There is a time to work and a time to play. There is a time for everything worthwhile (see Eccles. 3:1).

All the values derived from the experiences discussed in the foregoing paragraphs are enriched immeasurably by God through public worship. Many things happen in our souls when we worship prayerfully together; that is, when we sing together, give our tithes together, and rededicate ourselves to God together. Consider three things that happen when we are *motivated by the desire to join others in public worship.*

First, when we worship together prayerfully we experience the presence of God. Nothing is more important than this sense of God's presence and the inner witness or blessed assurance. This goes with us into our homes, our work, our play, and into all that we do. Worship services are not the only settings in which we experience the presence of God. But, along with our private devotions, they are among God's most gracious ways of making Himself available to us. In public worship we experience the biblically based means of grace.

> Jesus, where'er thy people meet,
> There they behold thy mercy seat . . .

Second, when we worship together prayerfully God helps us to recover our sanity. That is, we recover our Christian ideals and values. We get our priorities straight. Most of our time is spent in secular affairs in a world far removed from conscious reference to the things of God. And sometimes during the week we let the paltry standards and values of the world trample upon our desire to be what God wants us to be. But when we return to the community of prayer and faith, we behold again what God wants us to be and do. And we promise God that we are going to take another crack at this thing called Christian Living. Then we can pray in song with Charles Wesley:

> From thee that I no more may stray,
>   No more thy goodness grieve,
> Grant me the filial awe, I pray,
>   The tender conscience give;
> Quick as the apple of an eye,
>   O God my conscience make!

> Awake my soul when sin is nigh,
> And keep it still awake.

Third, when we worship together prayerfully, we receive again the inner resources for creative living and service. We receive what, as we have seen, Paul experienced when Christ became his Lord and Master. That is, we enter the supernatural realm of God's *empowering grace* which equips us to see life through with courage and faith. Along with this, we receive empowerment from the Holy Spirit to draw others into the kingdom through Jesus Christ. So when we worship together prayerfully, we sing,

> Set our feet on lofty places;
> gird our lives that they may be
> Armored with all Christ-like graces
> In the fight to set men free.

In summary, Christ does not call us to get rid of desires. He empowers us to bring all our desires under the supreme Christian desire—the love of God and neighbor (which includes ourselves). Christ did not come into the world merely to give us good advice. He came to give us the *power* to live for God and neighbor. Through prayer we know and feel that public worship is ordained by God for renewing us in Christ. Through prayer the Holy Spirit mysteriously turns Word and Sacrament into dynamic means of grace. For we experience again the presence and power of the living Christ in us. And Christ becomes our master-impulse at home, at work, at play, and in every arena of our life on earth.

PRAYER AND FAITH

Faith, hope, and love are the three abiding Christian virtues. Many things come and go. Faith abides (I Cor. 13:13). Therefore, faith is a key word in the vocabulary of every Christian. Faith is a foundational word in the Bible. In the New Testament, in particular, this word expresses what is at the heart of our soul's salvation. And faith is necessary in our ongoing pilgrimage as Christians.

What is faith? It is putting our absolute trust in God's pardoning, redeeming, and recreating power in Jesus Christ. On our side, faith means bringing our whole being, with the help of the Holy Spirit, to the experience of absolute confidence and trust in God's power to save, keep, and recreate us after the likeness of Christ. So the word "faith" here belongs not in the arena of general culture but in the unique dimension of the religious and Christian.

I have often heard people say that we must have faith to live at all. We have faith that the air we breathe is not contaminated with destructive gases. We have faith that our food—prepared unseen by us—is not poisoned. We have faith that the sidewalks will not roll up and hit us in the face. We have faith in the laws of nature and of human nature. And so it goes. All of us experience a kind of "animal faith." But this, though valid in its sphere, does not take us into the dimension of biblical faith. Indeed, when we think only in these lesser terms, we are sure to be shutting ourselves from the realm of faith as understood by Jesus and the apostles.

Why? Because faith in nature and human beings— though indispensable—does not come to grips with our moral and spiritual needs in their profoundest depths. This "animal faith" is not the doorway to the forgiveness of our sins. Nor do we receive from it the power over temptation. Even our trust in the best elements of civilization and culture moves on a different level from Christian faith whereby we are recreated by grace for the new life of service through Jesus Christ. For such faith does not and cannot take us into the life-giving relationship with God. The real issues of our souls—the struggles with sin, mediocrity, selfishness, loss of morale, indifference, anxiety and dread, tragedy and sorrow, meaninglessness and emptiness—are left unanswered by faith in nature and civilization.

For this reason Paul distinguishes clearly between putting our trust in the offerings of this world and holding fast to God. As he said, "for we walk by faith, not by sight" (II Cor. 5:7). What does this mean? It means that we do not place our ultimate trust in the things we can see, or taste, or handle, or in anything that is merely human, but in God alone.

Paul affirms that we must hold fast to the infinite goodness of God in Jesus Christ no matter what we have done, where we have been, or who we are. We are to trust God to pardon us and to pardon us absolutely. For "where sin increased, grace abounded all the more" (Rom. 5:20). We are to hold fast to God for the courage and power to see life through. We are to trust God to help us in all creative and worthy endeavors. And above all we are to trust God to bring us into a living relationship with Himself. Augustine summarized all this when he said, "I have learned, above all things, never to make man the foundation of my trust." But such faith does not come easily. It comes out of the agonies of struggle, doubt, heart-break, desperation. More deeply, it comes when the Holy Spirit moves in our souls as we pray. Paul knew this when he said, "Likewise the Spirit helps us in our weakness; for we do not know how to pray as we ought, but the Spirit himself intercedes for us with sighs too deep for words" (Rom. 8:26).

Suppose our problem is that we are sinners. We know it. Those who love us know it. God knows it. We feel that we are too unworthy to be loved at all by God. We feel that we cannot be forgiven because we are too unworthy to be considered for any benefit from God. When strong souls feel this way they are apt to start doing good works. They get busy and try to whip up some merit before God by their deeds. But those who persist in this error end up saying with Martin Luther, who tried to *work* his way into God's favor, "Nor would my conscience, even if I should live and work to all eternity, ever come to a settled certainty, how much it ought to do in order to satisfy God." He never saw the light until he read with new insight those momentous words: "He who through faith is right-eous shall live" (Rom. 1:17). Such faith breaks the chains of our self-righteousness and frees us to move into the new life of true righteousness with God.

No words can exaggerate the importance of faith in bringing God and us together. Here we are not dealing in mere intellectual reflection which—though impor-tant in its special function—has no power to save. Nor are we concerned with mere forms and ceremonies which, apart from faith, have no power to redeem or recreate. Nor are we referring to hard work, sacrifices, self-discipline, or moral duty, which, though having their proper roles, do not and cannot function to bring us to God. Even our willingness to repent and surrender ourselves to God falls dead without faith. Repentance and surrender are necessary. But the *power* of God comes by grace through faith. When we repent and hold fast to God's mighty action in Jesus Christ in our behalf, we are forgiven. Similarly, when we put our trust in God, we are conquerors over temptation. When we trust God to help us in a great cause for others, we receive His power, which enriches and enhances our otherwise feeble resources. Through faith God empowers us both *for* mission and *in* mission.

These abundant blessings become available primarily through prayer. For in vital prayer the soul ceases its merely intellectual, aesthetic, moral, ritualistic approaches and gets down to the essential process of opening itself to God. In prayer commitment is basic. And in authentic prayer the whole person—thought, feeling, will, desires and aims—is brought before God. And by the mysterious movements of the Holy Spirit, the soul is aided until it can take the leap of faith—of absolute trust in God's forgiving and empowering love in Jesus Christ. Then begins the new dimension of existence with God. All of this comes into being in the life of prayer where faith is born and nurtured. When we pray, faith thrives. When we stop praying, faith shrivels up and dies.

Therefore, we join the inspired writer who said, "And without faith it is impossible to please him [God]. For whoever would draw near to God must believe that he exists and that he rewards those who seek him" (Heb. 11:6).

PRAYER AND HOPE

Hope is the second of the three abiding Christian virtues. And in the New Testament it is given an emphasis unique in the history of religion. Christianity is a religion of faith and love. It is also a religion of hope. But, as in all of its major teachings, the roots of the Christian understanding of hope go back to the Old Testament, where the psalmists put their hope in God's faithfulness or "steadfast love which endures for ever" (see references on p. 31).

What is hope? It is the confident expectation of something marvelous in the future. It is the anticipated kingdom of God yet to come. In the Christian understanding, hope includes the desire for a worthwhile life for all people, as far as possible on earth, and also for a glorious life with God in heaven. So there are really two levels of Christian hope. One is the hope for a better life on earth. The other is the hope for a marvelous life in that new realm that we call the kingdom of heaven.

Here, I shall consider primarily the way prayer affects our whole attitude toward the future on earth. In a later chapter I shall treat the theme of prayer and the hope of heaven. What I have in mind here, then, concerns whether or not optimism about the future is based on reality.

The battle between optimism and pessimism has been fought in every society and in every soul. No one can escape this issue and, more than that, this personal struggle. Sometimes this struggle between hope and despair involves encounters with fatalism. There are environmental fatalisms, genetic or biological fatalisms, psychological fatalisms, and other sophisticated fatalisms. However contemporary they may seem to be, their advocates join their ancient forebears in saying: "No hope." But long after these fatalisms have come and gone, the story of the prodigal son, the glory of the Cross and Resurrection, and the miracle of Pentecost will remain to give hope to all who experience in prayer the power of God in Jesus Christ. When we think about the problem of fatalism and despair, we see that without God there is no enduring basis for hope. So when we leave God out of our lives, we place ourselves within the prison walls of an unremitting despair. To be without hope is to be "without God in the world" (Eph. 2:12).

Tolstoy, the Russian novelist, saw this. At a time when outwardly everything seemed to be going his way—when his wife loved him, his children respected him, his friends and relatives honored him, and the world applauded him, he fell into a profound despair. He could not understand how the peasants could sing or anyone be happy. By his own testimony he had someone hide the rope lest he tie himself to the rafters. He refused to go hunting lest he turn the gun on himself. As Joseph Fort Newton has put it, "He was a man going and not arriving, seeking and not finding; he was a God-haunted man." Tolstoy himself spoke of his experience as "a thirst for God." After two long agonizing years of searching, Tolstoy said, "God is that one without whom we cannot live."

We are like fish in ever-shallowing waters. We are like fish cast upon the shore beating out their life on the sands of an alien world. Then, if after all the futile flapping, one of them makes a final desperate lunge toward the sea, it finds an answering response in the element that gave it life. The psalmist expresses this thought in these words:

> My soul thirsts for God,
> for the living God.
> (Psalm 42:2)

On one side, the quest for hope must have intellectual foundations. For much depends on our total world-view. If we believe that nature (the physical universe) is ultimate, the best we can do is to "take refuge in heroic despair because ultimately we shall be crushed under the trampling march of unconscious power." There are two views concerning nature that are unacceptable to Christians. One is that nature is all there is. The other is that nature is self-explanatory. These views are not based on science. They are affirmed by those who simply assume that we live in a mindless, purposeless universe. And it is self-evident that they have no ultimate basis for hope.

When we believe in God, who has revealed Himself in the Bible, and who is affirmed by our best thinking, the theological foundation for hope has been laid.

But, on the other side, the practical basis for hope cannot be established theologically. Even when we believe in God but do not enter into the life-giving faith-relationship with Him, we merely overcome despair intellectually but not spiritually. *Life is deeper and more important than thought.* Therefore, we require both the theological and the practical answers to the problem of unremitting despair. How can this practical answer be found? In the Bible it is found through prayer and faith. This is more easily stated than experienced. For we are faced here with a persistent and dangerously destructive force in our lives. Pessimism is the swindling voice of Satan, urging us to give up our highest hopes and ideals and give in to our lesser natures. Nevertheless, through prayer and faith our deepest despair can be conquered. It can be defeated only when we enter and continuously reenter the faith relationship with the living Christ who is greater than all possible causes of discouragement.

But let us never be deceived into supposing that there is a one-time, one-moment solution to any serious form of pessimism or despair. Just when we feel free from its clutches, the demonic voice whispers in our ears thoughts of gloom and defeat. Therefore, we must employ the heart-principle of the devotional life: In returning shall be your strength. That is, we must return again and again to the Source of spiritual power and renewal, namely, the living Christ.

Our pessimistic moods are often brought on by our physical condition, body chemistry, loss of sleep, stress, sickness and other physical factors. Or, these moods may come from psychological pressures. They may have their source in the attitudes and actions of other people. They may result from catastrophic events which drain away all hope. More deeply and pervasively, unremitting despair may come from sin, wrong living, and the guilt that blinds us to the God of love, mercy, and hope.

Whatever shakes the foundations of our whole being must be faced. And the point is that, for the person who prays persistently and in faith, God is known to be the One who is unutterably greater than all the forces threatening our very existence. The prayers which thus bind us to God and make for hope need to be both private and shared. For to overcome pessimism and to live in hope, we need to share in the sustaining prayers of the community of faith and hope.

Moreover, in prayer that binds us to God we have the only sustaining basis for the deep yearning for *the ultimate triumph of righteousness.* The Christian faith satisfies this profound yearning. God reveals Himself both in the Bible and in prayer as the One who has already made provision for the triumph of righteousness. The Cross is followed by the Resurrection. Therefore, in those who pray in faith there is a present assurance of victory. For God is with us.

A faithful Christian is undiscourageable. This is not to suggest that we may not have our pessimistic moments. It is rather to affirm that through prayer in faith we overcome these moments by the unbreakable bonds with the God and Father of our Lord Jesus Christ. God does not create and sustain a magnificent universe and human beings capable of becoming bearers of His grace and then allow everything to fizzle out in the end. Degeneration cannot get the last word in God's universe.

Therefore, we join the ancient psalmists in saying that the steadfast love of God endures forever. With the angel Gabriel we too sing of the Messiah, saying, "Of his kingdom there will be no end" (Luke 1:33). And we join the "loud voices in heaven" in proclaiming: "The kingdom of the world has become the kingdom of our Lord and of his Christ, and he shall reign for ever and ever" (Rev. 11:15).

PRAYER AND LOVE

It is an axiom of psychiatry that we may truly live, if we truly love. This is to reaffirm what Jesus lived and taught nearly two thousand years ago. Love is the royal law of life. It is foundational in being a real person. And it is at the heart of our existence in the world as Christians. In this chapter we shall see that there have always been deep-rooted obstacles, both in human nature and in civilizations, that have blocked the way to Christian love. Therefore, prayer in the name of Christ is the divinely appointed way to Christian love.

What is this love? It is not merely human affection. It goes beyond our self-understanding. In order to see what it is, we require God's revelation of Himself as love. And the divine summons to love may be heard first through the Old Testament where God calls His children to holiness. God commands Moses to say to the people: "You shall be holy; for I the Lord your God am holy" (Lev. 19:1-2). This holiness code was taken up by the earliest Christians, who understood the meaning of holiness in the light of God's revelation in Christ (cf. I Pet. 1:16-21). Christian love is Christ at work in us for the glory of God and the blessing of others.

There are three decisive reasons why Christians hear God's call to the life of love. First, God is love and He requires us to live according to His purpose. The God of holy love gives the two great commandments, namely, that we are to love God with all our heart, soul, and mind, and our neighbor as ourselves (Matt. 22:37-40; Deut. 6:5; Lev. 19:18). Second, by His teaching and example, Jesus calls us to love. He manifested this call supremely on the Cross when He gave Himself that all who believe might have everlasting life. Third, life demands love. No one can truly live without it. For God created our human nature—with all of its levels and varieties—for love.

But we cannot weave into our daily living the love of Christ without God's help. Therefore, we are to hear the divine summons to pray for the grace to live the life of love. We are to pray in faith, confidently; for we know that the Father who commands us to love has promised with that command the grace to realize it. Therefore, when we go to God in prayer, we know that He is present to quicken our own resolve and to help us to manifest the love of God and neighbor. In this way we can carry out our Lord's summons to "let your light so shine before men, that they may see your good works and give glory to your Father who is in heaven" (Matt. 5:16).

The reason why earnest prayer is required for the life of Christian love is that it is not easy to love and to be loved. Again and again, we find ourselves lapsing into a disease of the soul which has characterized all civilizations, namely, the sin of looking down on others and consequently trampling upon them. The theme song of this awesome evil force in us is: "I'm up here and you're down there, and don't you ever forget it." All communities have been and are corrupted by it. It is one of the surest signs of our human depravity. It, together with the pride and greed which it implies, is the primary source of tyranny and oppression. Consequently, it inevitably brings on the awful scourge of "man's inhumanity to man."

This sense of egoistic superiority of status carries with it the conviction that it is right to trample upon others. This is the primary driving force of racial prejudice. In many nations across the centuries—where women have been belittled and "kept in their place"—it was the major cause of the exploitation of girls and women. Saint Augustine refers to "that notorious Lex Voconia . . . which prohibited a man from making a woman, even an only daughter, his heir; than which law I am at a loss to conceive what could be more unjust" (*City of God*, III, 21). But, bad as that was, it was trivial compared to the brutalities meted out to women and children around the world.

A recent documentary on justice in Brazil showed how, in some cases, husbands who murdered their wives have admitted their guilt and gone free. Why? Because the juries considered the supposed violation of the "honor" of the husbands as more important than the wives whom they murdered. No nations or societies are free from the injustices and brutalities which crush the souls and bodies of human beings for whom Christ died.

It is self-evident that there are vast ranges of inequality among human beings. We are not equal in talents, abilities, skills, self-discipline, physical strength, emotions, and will. Every father, mother, and teacher knows this. Nor are we equal in the privileges of birth and fortune. This elemental fact of life is a source of enjoyment and entertainment for people on all levels of life and ability. Regardless of our skills, position, and influence, we enjoy seeing, reading, and hearing the results of the achievements of outstanding persons. The masses applaud the performances of the stars. And all who can, seek out and pay for the services of great physicians, teachers, statesmen, writers, artists, composers, and athletes. All applaud those leaders of business and industry who develop successful enterprises which employ thousands of people and put bread on their tables.

And many are those who appreciate unusually gifted preachers.

But does this vast diversity of talents, skills, education, achievements—this extensive inequality among human beings—entitle anyone to look down on others or to trample upon them? Of course not. Saint Augustine stated his profound conviction, which he learned from sitting at the feet of Christ, when he said:

> No man has a right to lead such a life of contemplation as to forget in his own ease the service due to his neighbour; nor has any man a right to be so immersed in active life as to neglect the contemplation of God. . . . And, in active life, it is not the honours or power of this life we should covet . . . but we should aim at using our position and influence, if we have been honourably attained, for the welfare of those who are under us. . . . (*City of God*, XIX, 19)

Amid all the differences among people, we are all unutterably precious in God's sight. All of us stand in the need of prayer and grace. Before the issues of life and death and destiny we are all equal. And, at the foot of the Cross, we all kneel on the same level. People in positions of power and influence—as well as all others—need to pray for compassion. And what is Christian compassion but a feeling for others who are in misery and the desire to do what we can to help them? This is precisely what Christ brings, namely, the fellow-feeling which moves us to action. Jesus Christ came into the world to counteract the demonic forces of pride, greed, and superiority, which have been the chief sources of oppression and cruelty across the centuries.

I do not think that the effects for good of our Lord's teaching on the incalculable value of each human soul have ever been adequately treated in writing. Alfred North Whitehead touches on it in his chapter entitled "The Human Soul" (*Adventures of Ideas*, chapter 2). There he suggests that, after centuries of slavery, the idea of the soul gradually played a decisive role in its abolition. And wherever the influence of Jesus Christ is felt, the call to human rights is heard. It was the Nazarene, more than all others put together, who gave embodiment through His followers to the mighty theme of liberation by identifying Himself with "one of the least of these my brethren."

Jesus taught His followers to go against both our natural feelings and the generally accepted practices of the world in order to love the most needy. The outcasts, the lepers, the poor, the ignorant, the hated Samaritans, the sinners—all those who were in special need—were precious persons on whom He had compassion. The most difficult people to love are our enemies. In no society throughout the centuries— with some special exceptions—has love of enemies been acceptable. Yet Jesus made a special point of teaching His followers to love their enemies and pray for those who mistreated them.

Besides the love for the needy and for our enemies, Jesus taught us to learn, with God's help, to love ourselves and those dear to us. This too is not always easy. It requires God's help. It requires a lifetime of growth in understanding and affection in and through difficult circumstances. And it requires prayer.

By now it should be clear that when we speak of Christian love we do not mean a weak, sentimental, mushy feeling or mood. On the contrary, Christian love is strong, creative, courageous. It is the sustained desire or policy, born in us by grace, for God's best for everyone. This is never a merely human achievement. Therefore, prayer is a God-ordained pathway to Christian love. The Bible does not teach that we can love those in greatest need or love our enemies in our own strength alone. Jesus knew that we *could* not and *would* not do it. Saul of Tarsus, the great seeker after righteousness through the law, discovered that he could not be what God wanted him to be without the power of the living Christ. It was that power which enabled him to pray for his enemies, to love and care for "the saints," and to write I Corinthians 13. In the light of this, we can see why Paul gloried in Jesus Christ, through whom he became a conqueror over sin and adversity.

The mighty Christian affirmation here, then, is that through prayer God meets us where we are and drives out egoism, bitterness, hostility, and indifference. He does this by filling us with the mysterious, wonderful, divine love. And this love—which is the love of Christ—recreates us. Through prayer we are set on a new course in the name of Jesus Christ. We experience an almost unbelievable release from all the old fears and hostilities. And we become truly concerned for God's best for everyone, including our enemies. This does not mean that we want our enemies to have their way, whether right or wrong. That would be non-sense. Nor does it mean that we are to yield to their evil ways. That would be joining the forces of injustice and oppression. It simply means that we pray for God's best for all people.

It is no trifling matter to know by direct experience that love is the creative dynamic of life. We should never pass this by lightly. For this concerns the essence of Christianity. Paul knew it. Speaking from the heights and depths of his struggles and triumphs, he said that no matter who you are, or what you do, or what talents you have, or how much you know, or what your place in society is, if you do not have love, you are nothing. You are sounding brass or a tinkling cymbal. And nothing you do endures in the kingdom of God (see I Cor. 13). Strong words! But when we think about them we begin to get the message.

What Paul was reflecting on prayerfully and what we are wrestling with in our own souls is the phoney and inauthentic in contrast to what is of utmost importance. In prayer, then, through Jesus Christ we begin the great new pilgrimage toward an authentic life of love which puts us into the center of at least some ranges of service for those in need. As for our enemies, we hate their evil ways and still love them. We no longer have time or energy to waste on hostility. So we pray for those who mistreat us, we seek God's best for them as well as for ourselves, and go on to do all the good we can. Jesus did not stop to counsel with Judas even though he told him to his face that he was the betrayer. But He prayed for Judas as well as for the others when He said, " 'Father, forgive them; for they know not what they do' " (Luke 23:34).

I said that through Jesus Christ we enter upon "at least some ranges of service for those in need." Some people have the feeling that they ought to respond to every cry for help. But this is not possible. Some are experts at peacemaking, others at raising money for good causes, others at race relations. Some are effective at building life-serving institutions, others at creating great homes. Still others are specially gifted in witnessing and evangelizing. All Christians are called to serve, but not all are chosen for the same tasks. And though, through prayer and giving, we share in the total mission of the community of prayer, faith, and service, each has his or her own ways of concrete personal involvement in the life of service. All members are working parts of the body of Christ. And all are needed for responding compassionately to the urgent cries of human beings in misery.

But again, the biblical-Christian teaching is that we can do no great work of love apart from the grace of God. This is not to deny that many good deeds are performed by human beings who have not responded to the light of Christ. For all human beings are bearers of God's grace on one level or another. There is in everyone "the true light that enlightens every man" (John 1:9), and there is the "law written on [the] hearts" of human beings (Rom. 2:15). But since we are concerned here with the kind of love which is so frequently pushed aside by our pride and selfishness— as well as by the paltry standards of the world around us—we require the earnest prayers for the love of Christ in order to glorify God and to be a blessing to our fellow human beings. And, with these prayers, we are to pray that God will so sustain us in all good endeavors that we shall "not grow weary in well-doing" (Gal. 6:9).

Our prayer will be: "Help us, O God, to be imitators of Jesus Christ, to walk as He walked, to love as He loved, and to spread scriptural holiness in the Church and throughout the world."

PRAYER AND WISDOM

Among the books of the Old Testament three are often identified as "wisdom literature." The inclusion of these in the Hebrew Bible indicates that it was a part of their heritage to give a special place to practical good sense or wisdom. Often this wisdom is in the form of maxims that express the distilled insights of experience. Gerhard von Rad likens a maxim to "a precious stone among trinkets." He says, "The demand which it must always satisfy is that of brevity, of compactness, and yet of intelligibility, with, if possible, a clear graphic quality; in short, that of being easily remembered" (*Wisdom in Israel* [Nashville: Abingdon Press, 1972], p. 5). Some of the teachings of Jesus are in the form of maxims. In any event, the "wisdom literature," the teachings of Jesus, and the sayings of Paul and other writers of the New Testament contain the divine call to wisdom.

We know also from practical experience that we need to have working relationships with our bodies and minds, with the natural order around us, with other people, with social structures, and with foreseeable prospects. Therefore, to help us in this process of lifelong growth in wisdom, we are given maxims for our guidance. But, in view of our conflicting desires, our readiness to forget, and our gravitational pulls away from God and from what is best, mucl nore than maxims are needed. We need that inner transformation of our desires by the supernatural action of the Holy Spirit which sets us on course toward the kingdom of God and His righteousness. In short, we must pray for what Wesley called "scriptural holiness," what we called earlier the supreme desire of the Christian, the love of God and neighbor.

But while this love aims us in the right direction, we require something else, namely, wisdom. Therefore, we are called by God to seek wisdom and to pray earnestly for the help we need in pursuing it. This divine summons is heard especially in God's call to love. The love of God and neighbor implies the quest for wisdom. If love is of God, so is wisdom. Therefore, wisdom, common sense, insight, sound judgment— call it what you will—is an essential feature of Christian character.

Why does the love of God and neighbor imply wisdom? Because we do not know whether or not we are truly or effectively serving God and neighbor without wisdom. Christian love is purposive. It has a job to do. Christ came seeking the well-being of those in need. So the question is: How can the purpose or aim of love be realized? Granting the motivating force of love, the rest concerns ways and means. And this leads us to see the importance of wisdom.

If we say we love someone and yet keep on making foolish mistakes which adversely affect that person's life, what good is that love? Sometimes it is difficult to know who do more harm, the bad or the mistaken. Just because a person "means well," or just because one has "pure intentions," does not indicate a responsible love. The right motive, which is love, may issue in harmful deeds. We have heard the saying that the road to hell is paved with good intentions. The fact is that love implies wisdom and is apt to be merely sentimentality without it. A mother and father may "love" their children while doing (not responsibly assisting with) their elementary school assignments for them. But that kind of love incapacitates the children for solid achievements in reading, writing, and arithmetic. What could an enemy do that would be a greater obstacle to their children's future? People may "love" each other and be unwilling to seek wise counsel when they have demonstrated their inability to handle their deep and dangerous conflicts. What kind of love is that?

There are two basic problems in us which have to be faced. One is the age-old problem of pride and selfishness. Except for a legitimate self-interest, self-centeredness and pride strike against the revealed purpose of God for our lives. Paul, Augustine, Luther, Calvin, Wesley, and many others have called attention to the biblical teaching on this "radical evil" in human nature. But not as much has been said about the second problem, namely, the tendency toward bad judgment and folly. Yet, this also strikes against the revealed purpose of God for us. If love, or right desire, is the answer to pride and selfishness, wisdom and common sense are the answers to our folly.

I am not suggesting here that we shall ever reach a stage of perfect wisdom in this life. Even when we love God and neighbor, we are liable to make mistakes. Indeed, even when we love ourselves, we make mistakes. This is partly because we do not know—and often cannot know—enough about the situations in which decisions have to be made. Sometimes we think we have made mistakes when in fact there were no good options. Hence, whatever we may do will be followed by regrets. As we look toward the future, our vision is blurred. As we look back, our mistakes loom large to haunt us. But let us never forget that often we blame ourselves for decisions which might have been the best we could have done under the circumstances. Here the better part of wisdom is to forget our past mistakes—except to learn from them—and move into the future with the earnest prayer for wisdom. In all of these practical matters, the "law of the best possible" obtains. God Himself does not expect us to do more than the best we can. In the light of all this, we can see that God's call to wisdom requires both our daily and our lifelong response. And God promises His help because God is the Lord of truth and wisdom.

This calls for the habits of orienting our minds toward reality in practical matters. There is merit in the practice of consulting persons who know more than we do. This is what we do in relation to our physicians. And even when we do our best to seek the ways of practical good sense, there are times when we simply have to muddle through. In what areas are we called upon to manifest wisdom? In our family relationships, in the choice of schools, in the selection of a vocation, in our choice of a life-partner, in our work for a living, in our recreation, in all times of major decisions, and, above all, in our selection of the church in which we want to experience and express our love of Christ.

It might be supposed that the attainment of practical good sense is an easy matter. All we need to do is make progress day by day. But it is not so simple. Just as we require the grace of God to enter upon the new life of love, so we must receive God's help in overcoming our strong tendencies toward prejudice, stupidity, and folly. Not enough attention has been paid to the obstacles to wisdom. For if we do not know the obstacles, how can we come to grips with them?

In the Bible we find many statements that show a keen awareness of the seriousness of the evils brought on by human folly. One writer speaking for wisdom says, "All who hate me love death" (Prov. 8:36). We are told that those who love God "hate every false way" (Ps. 119:104, 128). Jesus spoke of "a wise man who built his house upon the rock" and of "a foolish man who built his house upon the sand" (Matt. 7:24-27). And He included in the commandment to love God the words "with all your mind" (Matt. 22:37).

Let us consider now some of the main obstacles to wisdom or common sense and then reflect on how prayer can help us to overcome them.

For one thing, our very pride and selfishness are major sources of folly. The ability to make sound judgments is often corrupted by wrongness within. This is why John Calvin said, "Our reason is overwhelmed with deceptions in so many forms, . . . stumbles at so many impediments, and is embarrassed in so many difficulties, that it is very far from being a certain guide" (*Institutes*, II, 2, xxv). David Hume said: "Reason is the slave of the passions." And it has often been observed that the clue to our inconsistencies lies in our emotions. How many wars have been fought because pride overcame wisdom! How many homes have been broken and how many lives destroyed because self-love trampled upon essential sanity!

Again, and closely related to this, is the obstacle of the closed mind. Here a person will not listen to any view but his or her own. A person who *will not* learn is no better off than one who *cannot* learn. This too is tied to our beloved egos. Whenever our ideas are challenged we try to defend them because they are *ours* rather than because they are true.

Another obstacle to wisdom and common sense is prejudice. Prejudice is holding to ideas on the basis of our likes and dislikes rather than on the basis of the facts. Who can estimate the disasters to people's lives which were brought on because they failed to ask the simple question: What are the facts? What good is it to say, "I love the Lord and I love my fellow human beings," then in the next breath to say of the members of another race, "You are inferior"? The question is: What are the facts about all of those involved? It all comes down to orienting our minds toward reality.

Still another obstacle to wisdom and common sense is what I call "the tyranny of the immediate present." What is immediately before us is so fascinating, bewitching, and compelling that we thrust from our minds any considerations for more long-range planning. We do this unconsciously or half-consciously, without realizing what we are doing. We are dazzled by the present, the now, by what is immediately before us. We have here what might be called a kind of *secondary intelligence* as distinguished from *primary intelligence.* I mean by this that secondary considerations—in this case what is immediately before us—blind us to the larger and more far-reaching concerns. Personal, national, and world disasters have often resulted from this kind of breakdown of intelligence. Such a breakdown of intelligence could lead to nuclear destruction.

One more obstacle to wisdom and common sense may be mentioned, namely, wanderings of mind. Wesley addressed the problems brought on by this in his sermon entitled, "Wandering Thoughts" (*Works,* vol. 2, sermon 41). This is a universal problem in our human nature and it has far-reaching effects on our practical judgment. We daydream our way through life. We are fascinated by our reveries, by sentimental hopes disconnected from concrete action, and the life of wisdom becomes impossible. In a kind of sleep-walking half-conscious way, we keep our minds from thinking, reflecting, asking pertinent questions. Our minds are often not oriented toward reality because they are lost in reveries.

Where does prayer come into all this? Before responding to this question, I want to make one point clear. I am not here referring to academic or theoretical intelligence. College and university work is important, and so is the work of scholars. But learned scholars and teachers are in danger of the pitfalls here discussed as much as the unlearned. Nor am I speaking of a high I.Q. When I speak of wisdom and common sense I am referring to *something everyone can attain* in some degree. But it requires the willingness to stop and think, to ask such questions as these: What are the facts? Am I overlooking something important? Whose judgment might help me here? Should I wait a day, a week, or a longer period before deciding? What will happen, if I do this or that? Any normal person can stop and ask such questions.

Marshal Foch, the head of the Allied Forces in World War I, said something long ago which ought to be remembered by us today and for the rest of our lives. He said that all great battles have been lost because of the neglect of obvious matters. So is it in life. Wisdom is needed in all areas of our lives. It is needed in planning each day. It is required in managing our interpersonal relations, in earning a living, in saving and spending money, in what we choose to read and see, and in the care of our bodies. Wisdom is needed especially in our understanding of the Bible, for it is our guide to life here and to heaven when we die. In all realms we need the inspiration and guidance of the Holy Spirit. But we need to pray especially for the Spirit to "reveal the things of God."

The enemies of wisdom and common sense are all around us and within us. But when we pray, we enter into a living relationship with *the God of truth*, who hates needless ignorance and who despises prejudice. So when we pray, we feel ourselves to be in the presence of the One who understands us, our fellow human beings, and all things as they really are. Hence, we pray to God and ask for His help in overcoming the obstacles to wisdom and to enable us to grow in the practice of orienting our minds toward reality.

Moreover, when we make mistakes of judgment and lapse into folly, in prayer we repent of our sin, ask God to forgive us, and decide to take another crack at using our God-given intelligence. In no case are we justified before God in saying, "Oh well, that was just an error of the mind, not of the heart." Both are sinful. In prayer, as we feel ourselves in the presence of the God of truth, we become keenly aware that breakdowns in intelligence and lapses in common sense are sinful. These too are morally wrong in the sight of God. So in prayer we repent before God for our folly and ask for His help in using the minds He gave us more effectively. Only in this way can the work of love be done.

Prayer helps also by keeping us from being overly remorseful about our mistakes. No one is perfect. Everyone makes mistakes and will continue to do so. The point is, with God's help, to reduce their number and their consequences. Through prayer we receive from the Lord of truth the encouragement and strength we need to improve ourselves in straight thinking. So we are reminded of the words of Scripture: "If any of you lacks wisdom, let him ask God, who gives to all men generously and without reproaching, and it will be given him" (James 1:5).

In prayer we behold the glory of dedicating our minds not only to our own affairs but also to the affairs of Christ and His Church. For there too wisdom is required in order to carry forward the Father's work. Both in this realm and in the ongoing of our lives one of our daily prayers should be: "So teach us to number our days, that we may apply our hearts unto wisdom" (Ps. 90:12 KJV).

PRAYER HEALING AND INTERCESSION

When we pray for the sick and for others in need, we are engaging in intercessory prayer. At its best, this high level of prayer is expressing to God our deep concern for others. In intercessory prayer, in the light of the biblical revelation, we are aware that God's love and energies go beyond natural laws and processes. The God who created the universe—and whose energies pervade it—transcends it. In intercessory prayer, our spirits are opened to the vast resources of God other than those of nature. Such prayer leads us directly into the realm of God's redeeming and healing grace.

But many people today find it hard to believe in intercessory prayer. Why? For one thing, they are convinced that they live in a universe of law. Events occur according to law. Things are what they are, and their consequences will be what they will be. So people are what they are largely because of the laws of sowing and reaping. Why then should we pray for the sick and for others in misery? In response to this way of thinking, we must insist that it is dominated by the idea that God cannot act except through the laws of nature. But this clearly limits God's energizing to the physical universe and fails to consider the possibility that God transcends and is incomparably greater than the universe which He created and sustains.

Some people today find it hard to practice intercessory prayer because, even when they believe in God, they are apt to think of Him as too great to make any changes in response to our prayers. After all, does not God have basic policies for His universe? Why should God interfere with these just because we pray for others? In any event, is not God too great to deal in the small details concerning human beings? In response, we must note at the outset that everything depends on whether or not, and to what extent, God cares for each of His children. God has revealed Himself in Jesus Christ as the Ultimate One who cares supremely for each person. And since it is His holy plan to work through human beings in expressing His compassion, He works through our prayers to bless others. The greater our God, the more He knows and loves each of us. And the greater our God, the more eager He is to summon us to prayers in behalf of our fellow human beings in need.

Another objection to intercessory prayer is that God already knows every human need and, since He desires our good, our prayers are not needed. For God will already do what needs to be done without our asking Him. For example, if a person is seriously ill,

God already wants to heal and restore. Our prayer does nothing that God is not already doing. But the trouble with this is that it overlooks God's revealed plan to bring in His kingdom by involving us in the process. God works through our hands and feet, through our hearts and wills, through our thoughts and minds, and through our purposes. God also works through our prayers in behalf of our fellow human beings. This implies that there are some things that will not happen without our participation. Therefore, God is continuously calling us to the kind of intercessory prayer which leads to action.

Does not intercessory prayer infringe on the privacy and freedom of others? Should God tamper with a person's right to live his or her own life? When we pray for others, are we not assuming that God should override their freedom? For example, when we pray for a friend or enemy to be converted, does not this imply that we have no respect for the other's freedom to decide for himself or herself? For if God answers our prayer by converting the other person, what happens to personal freedom? In response to this, there is nothing whatever about intercessory prayer which violates anyone's privacy or personal freedom. I may influence you, and you may influence me without any diminution of our freedom of choice. The plain fact is that we are all influenced by many forces external to ourselves. Nature influences us. Other people—including bad companions—influence us. Events influence us. The fact that, through prayer, God may influence us and others cannot be used as a sound basis for denying human freedom. We need all the good influences which God graciously gives us through the prayers of God's people.

When we turn to the great characters of the Bible, we find that nearly all of them believed in intercessory prayer. And they practiced it. In addition to Abraham, Moses, David, and the prophets, Jesus taught it and practiced it. The entire life and work of Jesus was a prayerful ministry of intercession. And, as we have already seen, next to our blessed Lord, Paul was the master exponent of the principle of intercession in prayer. Moreover, the outstanding personalities in the Christian heritage, almost without exception, were people who practiced intercessory prayer. Indeed, one of their most notable traits was their passion for the well-being of the souls and bodies of others which they expressed in prayer.

How can we explain the insistence of the biblical characters on intercessory prayer? And how can we account for the persistence of Christians in all eras in the practice of it? The basic answer to these questions is that people of faith have witnessed and experienced God's actions. They have seen the cumulative evidences of God's responses to their prayers for others. Here we enter into a realm of mystery. We do not know much about the laws of divine healing. But we do know that God can and does heal people both physically and spiritually. We do not know precisely how God can assist a person through the Holy Spirit in being converted and, at the same time, not tampering with his or her freedom. But we know that God does it. Our own life on this strange little planet is a mystery, but we live it.

There are many things about ourselves that we do not understand. For example, the mysterious influences of the human mind upon bodily illnesses—despite scientific advances in studies of the brain—are still like unexplored terrain. The possibilities of mental telepathy and its bearing on intercessory prayer are yet to be fully investigated. Moving beyond these mind-body relationships, when we consider the reality of the personal God who knows and loves us, we may begin to open our minds to the healing and recreating work of God's grace. The least we can do in these times of doubt is to maintain an openness to the possibilities and to the witnesses of God's mysterious interaction with us in making us whole.

Against this background, I see no adequate basis for giving up a strong faith in the efficacy of intercessory prayer. The laws of nature abide unchanged. When we pray for others, and when God answers our prayer, no known laws of nature are suspended. Rather, what happens is that the laws of interpersonal relations are brought into operation upon our human situation. That is, another dimension of God's energies is at work. This is the dimension of God's redeeming, recreating, and healing grace. The Christian claim is that in intercessory prayer some of the mysterious depths of divine power are released and made available to people.

But if God knows our needs and wants our best interests, why should we have to pray for others? Because God withholds some ranges of His grace and power until we fulfill certain conditions. Why? Because it is God's holy purpose, in His dealings with us, to work in and through us. To be sure, in many ways God takes the initiative to bless His children without any effort on their part. He sends the rain on the just and unjust, and provides sunshine for the good and bad alike. He creates and sustains us by His general providential care. But the point is that over and beyond these benefits there are those which come only from our intimate concern and involvement with each other and with God. These are the unique values and resources that come only as we are consciously and deeply related to each other in the love of Christ.

God wants the homeless to live in good houses. He knows that they need them. But He does not build houses for them. He works through people to realize His purpose that they be well housed. God wants peace on earth. But He does not bring peace unless people get together and work out their differences. In all that affects our human situation, God works through our minds, our words, our prayers, and our deeds. It is a law of the spiritual realm that God will not do for us what He expects us to do with His help. And our part includes intercessory prayer. It is simply a part of God's redemptive purpose for us to pray for one another. And thereby God accomplishes ends which would not otherwise be attained.

Another consideration here is that when we truly see and feel the need of others who are in misery, we cannot help but pray for them. When loved ones get life-threatening diseases, we can not help praying for them. When those we love miss the way, and miss their opportunities, we cannot help but pray for them. When we begin to understand the awesome possibilities of nuclear destruction, we cannot help but pray for those world leaders who hold in their hands the possibilities of war and peace. When we know that the church is in a sinful world, and, in many places, is suffering persecution, we cannot help praying for the Body of Christ. What is behind this driving spiritual force moving us into intercessory prayer? Surely the answer is the Great Heart of God who wants us to be bound to each other through the mysterious ties of intercessory prayer.

Intercessory prayer binds us to each other in love. It is a marvelous source of basic good will toward others. Praying for each other has deep interpersonal meanings. Moreover, it is the Christian conviction that God changes people and events through intercessory prayer. For example, if mental telepathy and extrasensory perception are possible, what is to stand in the way of divine-human interaction whereby every sincere prayer of intercession is answered through the transmission of divine suggestions and impulses? If God can put a thought into the mind of a person, God can answer prayer. If God can influence another by suggestions awakened through our prayers, God can answer those prayers. Similarly, if God, through our earnest and sincere concern for the physical health of another person, can release new spiritual and physical energies which affect his or her body, God can heal that person through our prayers. And these things have happened again and again.

Some words of caution are needed here. We are discussing things mysterious. We do not know the laws of God's interaction with us in the interpersonal processes of praying for each other. We only know that in these processes we meet reality.

We do not know the laws of divine healing. We affirm that God can heal anyone of any disease. And we affirm that all healing comes from God. God works through physicians, surgeons, nurses, hospitals, and through the patients themselves to heal. God works through changes in climate and physical environments to heal. God heals through changes in the attitudes of people. And God works through the prayers of caring people to heal. Biblical history and Christian history are filled with healings which occurred because of prayer. The following words of Scripture give witness to what has happened: "The effectual fervent prayer of a righteous man availeth much" (James 5:16 KJV).

It is with good reason, based on Scripture and experience, that pastors and congregations of all Christian bodies pray earnestly for the sick and dying. We know that all of us are dying. But we cannot believe that God wants anyone to die without our prayers. And we know that God does not want any human being to die prematurely. Therefore, we shall continue to pray for God's healing presence and power to restore the sick to health. We know that in many cases, despite all our prayers, the diseases continue steadily on their courses until even some of God's best children die prematurely. Nevertheless, we believe it is God's holy will for us to pray for healing of body and spirit; and we leave the rest to God.

In concluding this section, we may observe at least four ways in which God enriches His children through intercessory prayer. First, God gives all the values that we experience from a closer walk with Him. Such prayer binds us to God. Second, God blesses us by binding us closer to each other. In intercessory prayer God quickens and enlarges the love of neighbor. Third, when we pray for others in the spirit of Christ, we act to bring about what we pray for. We serve others. So when we pray for God to heal another, we try to find ways in which we can help in the healing process. When we pray for a person to be converted, we try to do what we can to draw that person into the orbit of the love of Christ. A fourth value in intercessory prayer is that, through it, God releases energies which would otherwise be withheld. God's grace flows through our intercessions.

Perhaps now we can understand better why God summons us to pray for each other and for the needs of the whole world. Jesus said, "The harvest is plentiful, but the laborers are few; pray therefore the Lord of the harvest to send out laborers into his harvest" (Matt. 9:37-38).

PRAYER AND COMMUNITY SERVICE

In the Bible, God has revealed His plan to realize His aims on earth through people. And this explains why all of us want to be a part of something greater than ourselves. God has given us the power to make choices about what we do with our time and energy. We can choose to work for God and with God. God has revealed also in the Bible that He has great expectations for each of us. Therefore, God calls us to realize His plan for us. That plan means taking the one life He has given us to join others in doing a great work. Our part may seem small. But we must remember what Jesus said about the kingdom of God. "It is like a grain of mustard seed which a man took and sowed in his garden; and it grew and became a tree, and the birds of the air made their nests in its branches" (Luke 13:19). When we work together, God turns small deeds into great blessings.

The major characters of the Bible called upon the people to work with God in community. They knew that human beings can actually share with God in doing a great work. There is an audacity about this that both startles and challenges us. Those biblical characters were adventurers with God. Abraham was called to establish a people under God. Moses committed himself to freeing that people from slavery and to forming them into a community under the laws of God. The prophets were called to bring back the forgetful people of Israel and Judah to the "rock from which [they] were hewn" (Isa. 51:1). Paul, with his missionary vision, went out to establish churches at the places that bear the names of most of his letters. To think of Corinth, Galatia, Ephesus, Philippi, Thessalonica, and Colossae is to think of the people there whom Paul formed into communities bearing the name of Christ.

When we glance across the pages of history and read of the important characters of the Christian Church, we become aware that they committed themselves to doing a great work with God. And we too feel that we would like to join them in the vast procession of those who lived and died as coworkers with God. How can we do it?

The starting-point is prayer. Why? Because only through prayer does the Holy Spirit move us into that total commitment which working with God in community demands. What happens in prayer that sets us on the path to this greater work with God? Three things. Many others; but consider three.

First, when we pray, we hear God's call to start traveling with Him. God is headed somewhere. He is, through and through, purposive. God has tremendous goals to accomplish in and through us. There is a legitimate place in *theology* for the analysis and understanding of the idea of purpose. It is useful, *theologically*, to show the absolute contrast between the biblical idea of the God who acts purposively and certain ancient and modern ideas concerning the aimlessness of things. The issue between a worldview in which purpose is ultimate and one in which blind chance or impersonal process is ultimate is perhaps the most crucial of all on that topic.

As far as the meaning of life is concerned, everything depends on what we believe about God's purpose. But even though we may believe in God and His aims, this is still merely theoretical and intellectual. Life is deeper than thought. So we require a way of entering into the living relationships with this purposive God and feeling with Him the joys of a shared work. How does this happen? In prayer we feel the divine pull, hear the divine call, and respond to the divine challenge. In and through prayer we are given that attitude of mind and heart that prepares us to work with God.

This work might be peacemaking. Or it might be working with others to help the homeless. It might be building up the church or working creatively in strengthening those institutions that serve people. It might be building a noble family heritage. God's purpose for Christians might take them into business, day labor, skilled workmanship, politics, education, home-building, medicine, the mass media, athletics, or numberless other worthy walks of life. But in all of these there is the supreme objective of glorifying God and being a blessing to people.

It is well known that Johann Sebastian Bach (1685– 1750) decided to compose all of his music for the glory of God. What if we did that with our talents? Whatever our abilities and circumstances may be, God calls us to live for Him as coworkers. This happens most basically as a result of prayer. For without prayer we are not apt to seek divine guidance. And without prayer we tend to think of a thousand different things and forget about seeking first the kingdom of God and his righteousness (see Matt. 6:33).

Second, when we pray we hear God's command to get rid of all unnecessary baggage. Nobody can travel with God when carrying needless burdens. John Bunyon's *Pilgrim's Progress* still speaks to us. The picture of Christian weighed down with the burdens of guilt, fear, cowardice, and other needless baggage is unforgettable. If you go to the Bunhill cemetery in London where Bunyan was buried, you will find carved on one side of his tomb a picture of the pilgrim bent over with the weight of sin. He cannot travel. He cannot do a great work. But on the other side of the tomb the burden is falling off and the pilgrim stands up ready to move. So is it in life. What baggage must we get rid of in order to do a great work with God in community?

The first piece of baggage we must rid ourselves of is an undue bondage to the past. Here we must pray for God's help. I enjoy reading about what our forebears did. I like to think of the great moments in Western civilization and in the cultures of the East. I am proud of the heritage of our nation. I am proud of family lines also. But we must do more than bask in the sunshine of the accomplishments of people in days gone by. We must *learn* from them. We must build upon them. It is one of the tragedies of our time that many people act as though there is nothing to learn from our forebears. Their minds snap shut to great ideas, great works, great affections, and great commitments of the past. They have never gained a taste for the best that has been thought and said and done in the world. They are lured away by passing fads and stimulating novelties. Consequently, they are lost in the trivialities of their own contemporaneity.

But on the other side of our willingness to learn from the past is our bondage to it. It is a tragedy of every generation that some are so devoted to the past that their minds are closed to those possibilities to which God is calling us for the future. We cannot move with God by "resting on our laurels." There comes a time when, without trampling on our heritage, we must press forward into the future with God. Our forebears themselves would have joined God in calling us to "build more stately mansions."

Therefore, we should pray for God to give us the courage to throw off the weight of an undue homage to the past. In this way we can move into the future with God and claim what He has in store for us and through us. In this context we can do no better than to reflect prayerfully on the words of Jesus: "No one who puts his hand to the plow and looks back is fit for the kingdom of God" (Luke 9:62).

Another piece of baggage we need to get rid of is an easy-going contentment with mediocrity. The trouble with most of us is not that we are so bad, but that we are so easily satisfied with mediocrity. No great work can be done with God unless we hold before us the vision of the best. We need to guard with care our thoughts, desires, and our affections. Therefore, we need to pray for deliverance from mediocre, petty, vengeful, and trifling interests so we can become involved in the kingdom of God and His righteousness.

One more piece of baggage that weighs us down and incapacitates us for doing a great work with God is a chronically negative attitude. I refer to the habit of mind according to which nearly everything is wrong and nearly everybody is out of line. Nothing is right. I am not referring to honest and constructive criticism. Rather, I have in mind the chronic croaker. The great need here is for deliverance from an awful and sinful burden. And the only answer is, through prayer and a basic decision, to receive the grace of God which releases us from the burden of a soul tormented by negativity. Then our spirits are freed to work constructively with God.

Third, when we pray for God to help us to work with Him, we hear His summons to live the life of sharing. When God confronted him, Moses knew he had to share his leadership with his people. Moses was the greatest character of the Old Testament. He was a prophet, and more than a prophet. He was a teacher, and more than a teacher. He was a law-giver, and more than a law-giver. He was a deliverer of a people. And, through the fearful struggles during the perilous journey toward the Promised Land, he shaped Israel into a people who found their identity under the laws of God. Because of God's call, Moses had to give up the pleasures and comforts of Pharoah's palaces and devote his time and energy to God's great work with his people. He was a man of prayer.

Above all, Jesus, the Son of God and Son of Man, "came not to be served but to serve, and to give his life as a ransom for many" (Matt. 20:28). His life and crucifixion represent the most sublime manifestation of self-giving love for others that this world has seen. Jesus Christ has inspired people in all walks of life, in all levels of education, in all ranges of social status, and in all races, to break the bonds of their slavery to selfishness and respond to God's call to serve. Jesus was supremely the man of prayer.

The religion of the New Testament is a divine preparation for the call of God to live for others. For God has revealed Himself in Christ as self-giving love. It is easy to talk about sharing our money, talents, time, and prayers, but hard to do it. And the first requirement is to be a person transformed by the grace of God. Then there is a built-in attitude, a disposition, a policy of sharing. This is part of what Paul had in mind when he said that "if anyone is in Christ, he is a new creation; the old has passed away, behold, the new has come" (II Cor. 5:17).

What have we as Christians to share? Many things, but look briefly at three. We are called upon to share our great beliefs. It makes all the difference in the world what people believe. And yet, we Christians—who have the greatest beliefs to share—neglect our teaching responsibilities in our homes, churches, and communities. We are to share also our great experiences. If God has done something important for us, we should tell others about it. Every Christian has something to say about what God has done and is now doing. But too often we do not share this with others. To be sure, we should avoid trite ways of doing this. But nothing is more interesting and helpful to others than stating effectively the great things God has done.

We need to share also in great causes for Christ. If we are to do a great work with God, we must identify some worthy cause that has been lifted up by the community of prayer and faith. And we must give ourselves to it. Some will serve one cause; others, another. But everyone needs to join others in church and community in some significant cause for the glory of God and the blessing of people. This implies becoming committed members of a local church. In and through the community of prayer, faith, and service, we nurture and enlarge our efforts to serve God. There we realize that the church of Jesus Christ has something unique to offer people. It exists for the unique mission of calling people to God through Jesus Christ. It offers salvation, pardon, and empowerment from on high. It calls us to hear God's call to receive the divine grace that motivates us to service. Only the church exists to carry out this unique holy mission of proclaiming the gospel of salvation and calling people to lives of unselfish service for the blessing of human beings everywhere.

No other institutions exist for this holy mission. Business establishments do not exist for it. Labor organizations were not formed for this purpose. Colleges and universities do not exist for this unless they are under the sway of the church. The organizations for the promotion of drama, the arts, music, and athletics do not exist for what the church was founded to do. Therefore, Christians are called to join in prayer and churchmanship to bring the succeeding generations the greatest of all blessings, namely, salvation and the new life of freedom and service under the lordship of Jesus Christ. Then we are set on our way, with God's help, to work for justice, peace, and the conquest of everything that strikes against the well-being of human beings.

PRAYER AND THE HOPE OF HEAVEN

There are solid reasons for believing in personal immortality. The Old Testament pointed to it. The New Testament taught it. Jesus affirmed it. The apostles proclaimed it. And above all, God revealed His plan when he raised Jesus from the grave. Therefore, against the background of that Easter morning, the following words of Jesus on the life everlasting have an abiding significance: "Because I live, you will live also" (John 14:19); "I am the resurrection and the life; he who believes in me, though he die, yet shall he live" (John 11:25). These words become meaningful in our experience during times of worship and prayer.

Besides these biblical foundations for the belief in the life after death there is another one that should be mentioned. The loving, caring God we worship is not a being who, after creating a magnificent world, would simply give up his faithful children to cold nothingness. Moreover, God, who created the universe and human beings for a purpose, who redeems people through Christ, who empowers them by the Holy Spirit, would not let all the value of these vast divine processes melt into nothing. It is absurdly illogical to think that a loving God would allow death to get the last word.

Death is no problem for God. Since God is wholly good and all-powerful, He will see to it that His faithful children enter into the life everlasting. Philosophically speaking, the main reason for believing in the life after death is based on the goodness and power of God. But our final ground is the Bible. God has spoken. And what God has revealed in His Holy Word, He will bring to pass.

In December 1987, at the sessions of the American Philosophical Association (Eastern Division), I met again Professor Charles Hartshorne, who for a number of years was a member of the department of philosophy at Emory University. He is generally considered to be the foremost exponent of process philosophy since Alfred North Whitehead. At the close of a lecture on immortality—to which he was a respondent—I asked Professor Hartshorne: Is there a process philosopher or theologian who believes in *personal* immortality? He replied: "I know of one who is trying to move in that direction." Then, after hesitating a moment, he added, "No. I cannot think of one." The idea that our souls contribute to the enrichment of God is good and sound as far as it goes. But the denial of *personal* immortality runs counter to the biblical revelation in Jesus Christ. And, as I think, it runs counter to our best thinking about God and His caring concern for us.

The practical question that arises now is this: How can the belief in the life everlasting become a dynamic force in our daily living? Often we need to *feel* the "reasons" of the heart where God speaks intimately, personally and intuitively. We need to feel within us the presence of the Risen Lord. None of these theological reasons brings home to our hearts the *experienced assurance* of God's plan to conquer death and to lead us into everlasting adventures with Him in heaven. So the question is: Granting the belief in the life after death, how can it be moved into the very essence of our existence so we *feel* its power and anticipate its glory?

The answer is that this comes through prayer. For as we walk with God and He with us, we enter into an *experienced relationship* which we feel and know cannot be broken by death. For God will not allow it. In the life-giving relationship with our heavenly Father, we receive the mysterious, wonderful assurance that He has claimed us for Himself both for this life and the next. *Our heavenly Father, who is true to us in prayer, will not be untrue to us in death.* In prayer, then, the belief in heaven becomes a living hope that shapes and colors our entire existence.

Through prayer also we gain intimations of what heaven will be like. Many people want to think of heaven as a place, a setting, an environment. They take the biblical images of the pearly gates, the streets of gold, the jasper walls, and the crystal sea literally (see, for example, Rev. 21:18, 21). To be sure, there is a true meaning here. What the inspired writer is saying, it seems to me, is that heaven is a new dimension of existence, unutterably beautiful and magnificent.

We cannot think of any life after death which does not have some kind of environment. Biblical writers speak of this as "a new heaven and a new earth" (Rev. 21:1; see also II Pet. 3:13). Jesus referred to the setting in these words: "In my Father's house are many rooms; if it were not so, would I have told you that I go to prepare a place for you? And when I go and prepare a place for you, I will come again and will take you to myself, that where I am you may be also" (John 14:2-3). The main point is that God will provide a new environment—called heaven—where His children can grow, adventure, and rejoice with God and with those who love God.

In prayer we learn that the environment is not the main thing. Heaven must be some kind of magnificent place. There will be the "many rooms." But most important, heaven is more than a place: Heaven is a mysterious, dynamic relationship with God that begins here and is nurtured now by faith. Heaven is also an opportunity for creative work and sharing. In prayer these deeper meanings of our life together with God in heaven move from the merely theoretical and abstract and into the experienced *now*. For, as Jesus said, "Truly, truly, I say to you, he who hears my word and believes him who sent me, has . . . passed from death to life" (John 5:24).

In prayer we come to understand that heaven is a new relationship of love for God and creative concern for others. It is joy in the presence of God. It is hope for opportunities with God. It is adoration of God. It is glorying in His presence. It is peace unspeakable. It is the neverending summons to growth and creative advance. All these and numberless other features of heaven are hinted at in prayer. And in prayer the sublime words of Jesus move deep into our hearts: "Let not your hearts be troubled; believe in God, believe also in me" (John 14:1). Through the inspiration of the Holy Spirit the biblical vision of heaven and our prayer life come together in a mysterious harmony.

There is another important connection between prayer and the hope of heaven. Through prayer, the anticipation of the life with God after death becomes a primary dynamic for service in the here and now. For some people the hope of a glorious future in heaven lures them away from the responsibilities of today. But this cannot happen in true prayer. For when we

Christians pray, we do so with Jesus Christ before us. We pray in His name. And we are concerned for the physical and spiritual needs of people now. To pray and to have fellowship with the God and Father of our Lord Jesus Christ—even as we anticipate heaven—is to identify ourselves with the needs of people whom Christ lived and died to save. Indeed, any authentic hope of heaven depends upon our love of God and of our fellow human beings.

So in prayer we glory in the future. For Jesus Christ, our Risen Lord, has opened the door for us to enter the portals of heaven and join the community of all "the saints." We celebrate, in anticipation, the heaven that was prepared for us from the foundation of the world. At the same time, we glory in the present. For we now experience with God, through Jesus Christ, the intimations of the heaven yet to come.

Paul brought all of this together magnificently when, after referring to the glories of the life to come, he reminded the Corinthians of their present duties. He said, "Therefore, my beloved brethren, be steadfast, immovable, always abounding in the work of the Lord, knowing that in the Lord your labor is not in vain" (I Cor. 15:58).

I like the words, "abounding in the work of the Lord." When, through prayer, we *experience* the vital hope of heaven, there is present in us the new dynamic for service to others. By grace we long to follow Jesus in being people for others, both in this life and in the life to come.